HOW TO CREATE
MEMORABLE EXPERIENCES
THAT BUILD BRAND LOYALTY

the art of
Seducing
your
Customers

John Boccuzzi Jr.

The Art of Seducing Your Customers: How to Create Memorable Experiences that Build Brand Loyalty

Published by Skipping Stones Publishing
Newtown, CT

The art of seducing your customers : how to create memorable experiences that build
   brand loyalty / John Boccuzzi Jr.
Newtown, CT : Skipping Stones Publishing, [2024]
ISBN: 979-8-9890192-0-5 (hardcover)
LCSH: Customer relations. | Brand loyalty. | Leadership. | Teams in the workplace. |
   Customer services. | Sales management. | BISAC: BUSINESS & ECONOMICS /
   Customer Relations.

Cover and interior design by Rachel Valliere, copyright owned by John Boccuzzi Jr.

The S.E.D.U.C.E. method is a framework to deliver exceptional customer experience. Because each individual will interpret, utilize, and put effort into the framework differently, there are no guaranteed results.

QUANTITY PURCHASES: Schools, companies, professional groups, clubs, and other organizations may qualify for special terms when ordering large quantities of this title. For information, email John@Boccuzzillc.com.

SKIPPING
STONES
PUBLISHING

To my wife Cynthia, who gave me room to dream and a safe place to land.

Contents

Bonus Content

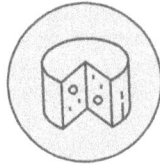

Scan the QR code below to
get a free download of
*6 Lessons in Customer Experience
from a Cheesemonger*

Introduction

Every moment of our lives impacts the choices we make, the loyalties we form, and the pathway we tread going forward. What do our lives consist of, if not a series of experiences fossilized in memories? First impressions are so powerful. They can change our lives through the people we meet, the places we visit, and the experiences we have. We sometimes don't even realize how much our daily decisions about what we do, buy, and consume are predicated upon these memories and impressions formed throughout our lives.

As a professional with a long career in sales and marketing, I have learned that our experiences of the landscape presented to us are paramount in building the sustainable relationships that are a bedrock of commercial success. We are more likely to spend our money on products and services where we have built a sense of personal investment. Brand loyalty isn't a question of resisting change (e.g., "I always wear Nike sneakers, and I always will.") We choose to wear that brand because we value the product and the ease with which it is bought, replaced, exchanged, and enjoyed. We embrace the "Just Do It" mantra wholeheartedly, just as Nike wanted us to.

While I may not have realized this at the time, it was during my childhood that I discovered the value of a powerful experience. Now, as an adult, precious memories from these early years have influenced the way I conduct my professional life. Details from our past are not always as true to reality as we like to believe, but this isn't important if the impression we had—whether positive or negative—prevails and is used to help us make informed choices going forward. The childhood memory that is most impactful for me is when I was taken to Walt Disney World by my parents at eight years old. My wife, Cynthia, and I have taken our children to Walt Disney World many times when they were young. I am sure if you asked them, they would have had the same magical experiences I had over 45 years earlier. The magic of Disney isn't something that can be pinned down to any one detail; it isn't the thrill of the rides, the sight of favorite Disney characters brought to life, or even the Mickey-shaped ice cream pop and hotdogs (which I can barely even remember). It was the sum of this, the whole experience. For my parents, it can be termed as the customer experience. I can forget for a moment what we did there, as the key is how it made me feel.

We didn't have a lot of money when I was a kid. You could say we were middle class, so we weren't staying in the expensive resorts. We had a humble, reliable green 1966 GMC pickup with an RV that sat in the back of the truck bed and over the cab. My parents, younger sister, and I all squeezed into this and slept like logs waiting to be fed to the campfire. I remember sleeping on what we affectionately called "the shelf," with the roof of the RV only three inches from the tip of my nose. Of course, you will no longer find me on anything but a king-sized bed with plenty of room, but as I think back to my time at Disney, I wouldn't have changed a thing. To get there, we'd drive 23 hours from our home in Connecticut to reach Orlando. As you can imagine, we all arrived exhausted. Regardless, as we pulled up to the campsite, we were pumped up on anticipatory adrenaline, raring to go.

The campsite was called Fort Wilderness. At roughly $19 a night, this may sound like a bargain now. But at the time, it was about $10 more than any other campground in the areas outside the Disney property. For our family, the vacation was expensive but affordable. It was certainly a treat, but for my parents, it was worth shelling out for. That's the thing about money; we are willing to part with more to get more. Value-for-money doesn't mean cheap and cheerful.

One thing I distinctly remember is that the campground was always spotless. There wasn't a discarded soda bottle or cigarette butt in sight. This wasn't just incidental; this was all centrally coordinated by the park. Disney wanted to create a wholesome family feel, and fields littered with garbage weren't part of their vision. Early on, Walt himself surveyed other amusement parks and noticed that people were more likely to drop their waste if they had to walk more than 50 feet to a garbage can. So, if you visit the resort today, you'll notice that you are never more than 50 feet away from somewhere to dump your litter. That kind of attention to detail may seem hypervigilant, but Walt realized that nothing should be overlooked when trading in people's future memories.

It's funny which details you remember. Of course, when you are trying to create good memories of your business or brand in the eye of your client, it's important to remember this is something that cannot be forced or shoe-horned in. Every part of the experience needs to be curated with a careful touch to cater to all the different perspectives that are being entertained. I remember the smell of pines from the large trees we parked under. I remember the spirit of the camp, something which cannot be manufactured in one fell swoop. There was the feeling that the families sharing the campsite each night were one big family together. I remember singing songs with giant representations of the Disney chipmunks, Chip and Dale. At the time, it never crossed my mind they were men and women wearing large, no doubt sweaty, costumes. Other things which I remember may seem ordinary or at least not specific to Disney, like roasting marshmallows by an open fire and making s'mores. The ordinary became extraordinary in the context of the whole experience. I really can't stress enough just how special those moments were. It wasn't just the campground that I remember fondly. I remember loving Chip and Dale, who would visit us every night. It felt so special that they'd want to spend their time with us when they could be at Mickey's house party or having dinner with the princesses in a fantasy palace. They were the nicest two chipmunks a boy could meet; one had a red nose and the other black, although I can't remember which was which. Every night my family would watch a firework display, the last dose of magic before I settled to bed on my shelf.

I am lucky to have had a very happy childhood. It's not that Disney was the only experience I remember fondly, but it certainly created a big impression on me. This is why years later I am still talking about it and taking my children to the parks. From a very young age, I was enamored by the opportunities and experiences that came my way. I wasn't spoiled and didn't have huge expectations about what my parents could offer me. I guess I was naturally curious and had a great spirit of adventure, and I think my experience at Disney is an excellent homage to my past. So, from the age of eight, which was my first visit (that I can remember) to Walt Disney World, I have been aware that great experiences can be offered without vast wealth or privilege. And those designing these experiences don't have to spend vast sums to enhance them. Often, it's the inexpensive details that make it. If you had asked my eight-year-old self why I loved Disney so much, I think I would have answered, "I just do." I wasn't being hard sold a single product. There wasn't any one thing to tempt my family. There was no special offer or free gift, but my memories are more valuable than any plastic souvenir.

Disney represented more than a family vacation; it represented the idea that regardless of your wealth, you'll be treated like everyone else. When you walk through the gates of Disney, there are no questions about diversity, wealth, or politics. Everyone there becomes equal under the same magical experience. As soon as you enter, your worries from your day-to-day are eclipsed as your senses are taken in by all the color, sound, fun, and laughter without any room for any insecurity or prejudice. This, right here, is one of the most important lessons for businesses in the 21st century. So, what is it about the Disney business model that has earned it so many words in the introduction to this book? Well, the resort nails customer experience, and with that, it attracts all the customers that have made it the multi-billion-dollar company it is today.

If the product or service which you sell isn't an exclusive commodity, you must rely on more than supply and demand to ensure customers are spending their money with you and not a competitor. We live in a global world now, so there's a lot more competition to fight off. A hundred years ago, you could create a widget in Connecticut and be incredibly successful because, quite frankly, you were the only widget vendor in town. There was no internet, and people weren't going to travel out of state to get that product if you sold it down the road from them. Gone are the days when you only had one place to shop, the we-sell-everything general store that met your needs without necessarily providing choice. But with capitalism, we have choice, and with choice, we have competition. Now, if I want to buy milk, I don't have to rely on that one shop. I could go to Stop & Shop, Trader Joe's, Caraluzzi's, or even Amazon and have it delivered to my house. The same product is available at multiple places, so the consumer is king. We decide where to spend our money, and your job is to make your business the most attractive option.

So, other than price tweaking and flashy (and often expensive) promotions with short-term impact, how can a business differentiate itself from the rest of the market? That's right, you guessed it—it's all about the customer experience you provide. Was the milk chilled? Was it available when I wanted it? Was the checkout process quick? Was it ethically sourced? Were there different brands I could choose from? Did the cashier ask me how my day was going? Was the store clean, or was the app easy to navigate? The list is almost endless, and checking a fair few of these principles off your list is going to give you an edge. So, suddenly, customer experience becomes a differentiator because, let's face it, milk is milk. It's got X amount of fat in it and it probably comes from a cow (or goat, nut, or oat these days). You get the idea. Cow's milk is cow's milk and oat milk is oat milk, whichever way you bottle it.

Therefore, the only thing differentiating that milk is the customer's experience while purchasing it and the story behind it. Every minor detail will make up the customer experience, which subconsciously pushes them to buy milk from store A and not store B, or from supplier C and not D. So from Mickey Mouse to the stuff we put in our morning coffee, we as consumers are more influenced by our customer experience than anything else. Extravagant television advertising and on-point branding adds sway, but if the customer's experience (having been drawn in by the noise of the media) is rubbish, then those nicely packaged products are going to collect dust on the supermarket shelves.

So, what's my point? Essentially, the power of customer experience should not be underestimated. This crucial part of business management must be maintained; after all, consumers are a fickle bunch. I recently became the happy owner of a Volvo after being a loyal and unwavering Nissan owner for 20+ years after an incredible buying experience (more on this later…). I'm writing this book to share these personal experiences and give you a better insight into why customer experience is so central to business success. What better way to start than by sharing my success story, right? When I co-founded my first software company, Kenosia, back in 1998, I brought on the first four customers (Schering-Plough, Dannon Water, Heinz, and First Brands) without having written a line of software code. Risky, I know. All I had was a PowerPoint presentation that looked like software but, crucially, wasn't. So, I was essentially trying to get customers before I had the product. I wanted to be sure what we were creating was worth buying. Bit of a long shot, but it paid off. Those four clients wrote checks to help us fund the software that they could use once it was developed.

Heinz was the first company to receive the software post-development; it was an exciting and yet nerve-racking time for all of us.

My nerves were well-founded. Not long after sending the product on a CD-ROM, I got a call from Heinz saying that they'd put the disc in their computer but nothing happened. "Houston, we have a problem," I thought. Thinking back about the power of first impressions and valuing the stature of Heinz as our first client, I pulled out all the stops. I told them we'd have someone fly down to check it out within the next couple of hours. We flew an engineer down to Pittsburgh that afternoon. As it happened, the expense of flying an engineer 500 miles could have been avoided. It soon transpired that it was a security block at their end that was preventing our program from working, an issue which was quickly resolved. Because this was our first client and we wanted to ensure an outstanding experience, we decided not to charge them for the cost of the flight or the engineer's labor. Good intentions are often rewarded, and this was true for us. The next week Heinz sent us $5,000, far more than we had spent trying to rectify the problem. From that point onwards, the business was a huge success; although I always valued the experience, we offered our customers more than just great technology. We offered an experience that they could depend on. One of the top industry publications at the time, *Consumer Goods Technology*, named Kenosia the #1 customer experience software firm two years in a row.

Incidentally, Heinz remained a client until we sold the firm 10 years later, proving the point that building trust with your clients by offering a fair and helpful experience is worth more than the cost of fixing mistakes that would otherwise be left to fester. Had I charged Heinz a fee for the travel and time, I am certain they would have paid. But would they have remained a customer for so long? We were investing in their loyalty.

In this book, you are going to learn how providing exceptional customer service can not only be the biggest differentiator in your business but how doing it well will cost you less up front and earn you more long-term than you ever thought possible.

chapter 1

The History of Customer Experience

S.E.D.U.C.E.

Providing excellent customer service is now a necessity in business strategy. Throughout this book, I will share personal stories, case studies, and a whole load of history to show you how to satisfy your existing customers and reel new ones in. Consumers are offered more choices than ever, so their expectations cannot be ignored. Any business looking to develop, grow, compete, and profit in today's marketplace needs to seduce their customers (**S**tep up; **E**mploy; **D**esign; **U**ncover; **C**onnect; **E**xpect).

Before we review the components of **S.E.D.U.C.E**, let's first delve into the history books. By understanding the history, we can better understand which foundational best practices have helped shape customer experience and how we can best leverage what's been learned. Let's start with the fundamentals.

The word "customer" originated in the late 14th century. (Who knows how you did your shopping beforehand?)

> Customer, "customs official, toll-gatherer" c. 1400, "one who purchases goods or supplies, one who customarily buys from the same tradesman or guild…".[1]

Likewise, the word "experience" also originates from the late 14th century.

> Observation as the source of knowledge; actual observation; an event which has affected one… from Old French experience.[2]

Of course, prior to the existence of these words, people did trade and purchase goods and services, which constituted an experience. However, it clearly wasn't seen as important enough to be defined. Nevertheless, these fundamentals of consumerism were added to the lexis hundreds of years before the inception of the capitalist playground we live in today.

Customer experience is an ancient practice, which is something my family and I learned a few years ago during a family vacation in Pompeii, Italy. During a tour of the ancient city, our guide described how street vendors would sell soups and other hot beverages to residents and visitors. Modern-day archaeologists have discovered remnants of vessels from which food was served with evidence of pork, lamb, snails, and other goods traceable on them. Paintings have been discovered depicting trade stalls filled with vessels with images of the product painted on the outside. This demonstrates that branding was used as a

---

1 Etymonline. "Customer." https://www.etymonline.com/search ?q=customer.
2 Etymonline. "Experience." https://www.etymonline.com/search ?q=experience.

marketing tool long before modern giants such as Coca-Cola and Apple excelled in this area of branding and customer experience. This all got me thinking. These Greek (prior to Pompeii becoming a Roman city) vendors must have needed a strategy to try to out-sell their competition, just like businesses do today. Maybe it was the unique lamb, fish, and snail combinations they offered or the unique blend of spices they used (long before KFC got on that bandwagon). Perhaps it was simply a battle of competitive pricing or how they greeted their customers, possibly trying to learn the names of regulars. Whatever tricks they did employ, they are most likely much the same as many of those used today. As I looked around the ruins of Pompeii, I began to imagine the powerful sensory experience enjoyed by those navigating the bustling streets over 2,000 years ago. I thought about the 13,000 residents of Pompeii: men, women, and children all occupied with their busy days, overlooked by the awesome beauty of Mount Vesuvius—a natural phenomenon that would ultimately engulf their spectacular city. I imagined the smells of the hot soups, grilled meats, and beverages; the sounds of people trading, bargaining, and sharing stories of the day; the feel of cobblestones under their sandals, the comfort of soft fabric togas against their skin; and the smooth granite counters from which the refreshments were served. As I imagined all this, it felt like I was experiencing this world myself. In reality, these vendors weren't so different from owners of modern-day street carts or food trucks that we see in major cities like Los Angeles and New York City today.

Why is this relevant? Well, the customer experience is about atmosphere and ambiance as much as anything else: location, prices, smells, feelings, textures, sights, sounds, and the interaction with the owner or employees. Certainly there were customer experiences earlier than ancient Pompeii, but I think 2,000 years ago is a good place for us to start.

A big difference between 2,000 years ago and now is that the consumer would have had far less choice and, equally, the vendors fewer potential customers. Among the residents of Pompeii, you had the poorer classes and slaves who wouldn't have had the social status or means to be popping into the ancient equivalent of Starbucks. This was a world with no mail order, no internet, much less tourism, and certainly very few global travelers. The customers who were able to buy pre-made food were limited to what was available in their location; supply and demand wasn't the force it has become. Nevertheless, it would have only taken a second soup vendor setting up shop to potentially steal all your business. Therefore, there still must have been an advantage to creating memorable experiences that would keep patrons coming back. Memorable doesn't necessarily mean a good memory, mind you. I like to think that some of these vendors were like the "Soup Nazi" in the TV series *Seinfeld* or Dick's Last Resort and Wiener's Circle, both in Chicago, where waiters are surly to customers on purpose. But if your main rival was located several miles away, it didn't always matter.

Another example of customer service from ancient civilizations was also made apparent during that same family holiday in Rome, Italy. As we arrived in Italy's capital, it was impossible to ignore the magnificent structures built by the hands of men and women living over 2,000 years ago. Unfortunately, the ingenuity of the Roman Empire was built off the back of slave labor, which is a sad reality that should always be remembered. Shockingly, modern-day slavery continues to be an issue around the world today. The garment, shoe, cotton, and electronics industries are some of the biggest culprits. Sadly, the United States is listed in the top 10 nations with the highest number of people living in modern slavery. India, China, North Korea, Pakistan, Russia, Indonesia, Nigeria, Turkey, and Bangladesh make up the other nine. Six of those countries are in the G20.[3]

That aside, the Coliseum is a truly beautiful work of art, architecture, and engineering. It is visited by six million tourists every year. What's more interesting is that it took only eight years to build without any of the advantages of modern technology. In its heyday, this venue hosted as many as 50,000 spectators and was used for over 500 years! A modern equivalent would be Madison Square Garden (MSG). Despite being built as recently as 1968 (taking 245 days to complete), MSG is the oldest sporting arena in metropolitan New York. The arena's maximum capacity is 20,889 spectators, less than half of that of its ancient predecessor.[4] Both venues are famous for hosting epic battles, but thankfully the prize boxing fights of our modern era are somewhat less brutal than the gladiator fights in Rome.

So, what is the connection between customer experience and the Coliseum? Well, just like the big boxing promoters, Emperor Titus had a huge arena to fill. From the gladiator fights to criminal executions, Titus ensured that there was always something exciting to witness within the walls of the arena. They even designed the space to fill it with water so ships could battle within. MSG does accommodate an ice rink, basketball court, and the arena Billy Joel calls home, but that's not even close to as impressive! The fact is, without an exceptional customer

---

3 Gottbrath, Laurin-Whitney and Feng, Alice. "Compounding Crises Push More People into Modern Slavery, Report Warns." Axios. Accessed August 21, 2023. https://www.axios.com/2023/05/25/modern-slavery-countries-rank-list-forced-labor.

4 Esteban (October 27, 2011). "11 Most Expensive Stadiums in the World."ssS Total Pro Sports. Archived from the original on August 27, 2012. Accessed July 2023. https://en.wikipedia.org/wiki/Met Life_Stadium.

experience, they would not have been able to get bums in seats for half a millennium. The average population of ancient Rome was just one million, which is dwarfed by the population of New York City, which is eight million and counting. At full capacity, the Coliseum could host 5% of the population, and there weren't private jets flying in wealthy visitors from out of town. You get the picture; the Coliseum was a triumph, even by modern-day standards. Nothing can stand the test of time without, at the very least, a memorable customer experience.

Let's put our loincloths back in the closet and fast forward 1,500+ years to 1907 and the opening of the first Neiman Marcus department store in Dallas. The company was started by Herbert Marcus Sr., his sister, Carrie Marcus Neiman, and her husband, Abraham Lincoln Neiman. Their mission was to bring high-end clothing and fashion to Texas (Stetsons were optional).

The store and business model were an instant success, and come the 21st century, they are now a multi-billion-dollar enterprise. Today the Neiman Marcus Group operates six brick-and-mortar stores, two Bergdorf Goodman stores, five Last Call stores, and an online retailer for home furnishings, "www .horchow.com."[5]

I mention Neiman Marcus because their attention to detail, salesmanship, and customer experience is legendary in the world of retail. In fact, Stanley Marcus, son of Herbert and former president of Neiman Marcus, became known as "America's Merchant Prince." Stanley was focused on exceptional training for his staff and the prioritization of his customer. He once famously complained:

> I am unaware of any store, or any business school,
> for that matter, that conducts a course or a series of

---

5   https://www.neimanmarcusgroup.com/our-brands. Neiman Marcus Group. Accessed August 3, 2023.

lectures on the care and treatment of customers. I am referring to "customers" and not "consumers," for never in my retail experience have I ever seen a "consumer" enter a store. I've seen lots of "customers," for that's what they call themselves.

It may seem like he is simply arguing semantics, but his distinction is more valuable than that. The term "consumer" is impersonal, calculated, and procedural. The focus is on the act of "the one who purchases," whereas the term "customer" can be applied to an individual and is often used in conjunction with how they feel—"a satisfied customer," for example.

For Stanley, customers were never an afterthought, as he prioritized customer experience above everything, including profit.

"You're really not in business to make a profit, but you're in business to render a service that is so good people are willing to pay a profit in recognition of what you're doing for them."

Neiman Marcus purchased Bergdorf Goodman in 1972; this high-end store appealed to Neiman Marcus's customer base by also focusing on providing an exceptional customer experience.

In 2007, I was lucky enough to meet Ira Neimark, the former CEO of Bergdorf Goodman, after being introduced by my friend, Pamela Miles. At the time, Pamela was the executive assistant to Jack Mitchell, the CEO of Mitchells Richards & Marsh, three ultra-high-end retail stores in Connecticut, Long Island, and New York known for top-tier customer service and experiences (more on Jack and his incredible retail business later). From that first meeting, I knew Ira and I would be friends, as he immediately became a mentor to me.

Ira was 86 when we met, but you would never have known it. At 86, he was still lecturing at Columbia University, and I was fortunate enough to sit in one of his lectures. He even introduced me to the class and allowed me to share a few observations on customer experience with his students.

Over many lunches together, Ira would tell me stories about brands like Ralph Lauren, Fendi, Haute Couture, Yves Saint Laurent, Hubert de Givenchy, and Christian Dior, to name a few; his market knowledge and experience were second to none. During his dealings with these big fashion houses, his contacts weren't just business representatives but the very people the brands were named after. Ira was even responsible for introducing several of the European brands to New York City for the first time and capturing exclusives for Bergdorf Goodman.

One of his stories, which I remember fondly, concerned the time he met with Ralph Lauren to convince him to break his exclusivity with Bloomingdales in New York City and sell his titular clothing line at Bergdorf. Mr. Lauren was not convinced that there was enough distance between Bloomingdales and Bergdorf to merit the expansion, so Ira ended up hiring a helicopter to take them both above the city to see the distance between the two stores. When they landed, Mr. Lauren agreed to expand his line to Bergdorf.

You can read about this story and dozens of others in *Crossing Fifth Avenue to Bergdorf Goodman: An Insider's Account on the Rise of Luxury Retailing*, a book Ira published in 2007, the same year we met.[6]

Ira was CEO of Bergdorf from 1975 until he retired in 1992. Under his leadership, Bergdorf's value grew from $18 million to over $250 million. It's fair to say that Bergdorf's success is partly reliant on its location on 5th Avenue, which is one of the most expensive shopping streets in the world. But it's also fair to say

---

6 Neimark, Ira, *Crossing Fifth Avenue to Bergdorf Goodman: An Insider's Account on the Rise of Luxury Retail 2nd Edition* (GamePlan Press, 2014).

that only a business that is successful can maintain a presence in such an exclusive location. As this geography comes with certain expectations, this is a place where commercial trade becomes a memorable experience. It was Ira's hard work and attention to detail in every part of the store that has allowed Bergdorf's to be a 5th Avenue success story. This detail included everything from the exclusive European brands available at Bergdorf's to the highly attentive sales associates who engaged with customers and took pride in their work. For patrons of luxury stores, the price of the goods is of secondary importance, and Ira knew this long before research confirmed that customers were willing to pay more for an exceptional customer experience. The power of customer experience has so greatly influenced market movement that PricewaterhouseCoopers (PwC) now publishes an annual customer experience report. In the 2022 report, they calculated that customers are likely to pay as much as 16% more for exceptional customer experience. While it's easy to see how good customer service can lead to more sales than your rivals, Ira was also very aware of the opposing reality: bad customer service can lose you customers—brand loyalty is far more quickly lost than won. The same PwC report states that 33% of customers will leave a brand they love after just one bad experience.

In 2018, I was on a trip to Sweden with my wife Cynthia and our two children, John III and Sabrina, to pick up our new Volvo XC40 from the factory in Gothenburg (I promise I will tell you that story soon!). Checking my voicemails, I had a message from Ira. Although he was keen to meet with me, it was not to be. Sadly, he soon passed away at the ripe old age of 97. While it was a great shame that I never got to see him again in person to enjoy his wise words one last time, it felt poignant that he'd left his voice with me so soon before his passing. I listen to this voicemail from time to time as Ira's voice reminds me of the example he set—living life to the fullest and always focusing on creating memorable experiences. He was successful in doing that for himself, his employees, his employers, and for the customers he served.

Although the words "customer" and "experience" originated in the 14th century, it wasn't until the 20th century that the two joined forces. In 1994, Lou Carbone coined the phrase "customer experience." Two thousand years after the soup vendors of Pompeii, the concept which defined their practices was brought front and center in an article published in *Marketing Management* (winter edition) entitled "Engineering Customer Experience." Carbone had formalized what Walt Disney, Ira Neimark, Jack Mitchell, and Stanley Marcus had already dedicated their working lives to.

His article shared the secret of creating customer experiences for a new generation of brands. However, almost 30 years later, it is astonishing to see how few brands prioritize customer experience. So many enterprises still have a business model which aims to minimize expense to maximize profit—which is shortsighted. Lou describes the experience as "the takeaway from an interaction with a brand, product, service, or business."[7] This takeaway is composed of all the impressions that customers form; some are subliminal, some are extremely obvious, some are designed with intent, and others arise from chance. Carbone describes two types of clues that create these impressions: performance-based and context-based. The former relates to the function of the product or service. But, how well does it do the job it is designed for? The latter relates to the appearance, demeanor, or presentation of the product or service received.

---

7   Carbone, Lou, *Engineering Customer Experience* Vol. 3, No. 3 (Marketing Management, 1994).

He then breaks context-based clues into two further categories. The first of these is "mechanics," which refers to sight, smell, taste, sound, and texture. The second category is "humanists," which refers to value emulated from people, such as friendly servers who remember your name. Ultimately, the game is to ensure the sum of all the clues presented to a customer leads to an overall net positive experience. No single detail can have the same lasting impact as the sum of all the impressions formed.

As promised, let's go back to Jack Mitchell. In 2006, I was the CEO of Kenosia, a small software company that sold to some of the largest brands in the world including Procter & Gamble, Nestle, Bacardi, Heineken, Mars, Coke, and Pepsi. I needed a few new suits and blazers, and my brother-in-law suggested I visit Richard's in Greenwich. He warned me that it wasn't going to be cheap, but the customer service and attention to detail they offered was like nothing he had seen from a clothing shop before. Ultimately, it was definitely worth the extra investment.

My first visit was nothing less than jaw-dropping. Upon entering, I was greeted by a welcoming associate. I told him that my brother-in-law, Mike Cairo, had recommended them to me. To my surprise, they didn't just pass on their gratitude. They asked me how he was doing before asking the same of my sister Marie. It felt like I was meeting friends of the family.

Then, after the small talk, I was treated to a wonderful cup of coffee. It was just what I needed. Then I enjoyed the experience of trying on some amazing blazers and suits. The experience left me in awe of their service, so I decided to learn more about Richard's and how they had developed such a successful enterprise. They are a high-end store, so competitive pricing isn't their differentiating factor. Much like Ira and Bergdorf, Richard's knew how to create a unique shopping experience through an incredible assortment of brands and exceptional customer service. As I researched the company, I quickly discovered that Richard's was owned by a gentleman named Jack Mitchell and his family. At this time, Jack's family also owed Mitchell's of Westport. He was the author of a book called *Hug Your Customers*, which I read within just two sittings—not because it was short but because I was thoroughly captivated from start to finish. The book had so many valuable lessons that I was keen to share with my clients. This was when I first met Pamela Miles, his executive assistant at the time.

She helped me secure 100 signed copies of Jack's book and arranged for me to meet him. Jack was full of enthusiasm when I met him in his store in Westport; he was proud of his store and was eager to show me around. As we wandered around, I could see that every part of his creation was inspired by his dedication to an enhanced customer experience. I remember Jack telling me how he had a printer installed in his bedroom which was directly connected to POS (point-of-sale) data. Every morning he would print out a list of all the customers that spent a considerable amount of money in the store and send them a personal thank you note, all before he left his bedroom. Absolutely incredible.

There are stories like this in his book *Hug Your Customers* and the sequel *Hug Your Employees*, both of which I thoroughly recommend.

Jack, like Ira, became a friend and mentor. I became a frequent shopper at his store in Westport. During each visit, someone would greet me. That person was usually Joe Derosa, who became my personal salesperson. He would always ask how Cynthia and the children were doing, making me feel like more than just a consumer—I was a valued customer. Yes, he had a great memory, but Jack had also set up an incredible CRM solution long before

Salesforce came to market to profile and track each customer. A customer's favorite brands, how much they were comfortable spending, family details, hobbies, and favorite sports teams were all noted and absorbed by sales associates.

On one visit, I was browsing through a rack of suits that were part of a new display when Joe approached me as if he was an old friend. He politely suggested that I may appreciate the suits on another rack even more. In fact, what he was doing was redirecting me to the suits that were more in my price range so I wasn't put off by the higher prices before me. In another store, I may well have been left uncomfortable and embarrassed at the prospect of spending more than I had budgeted for. I may have either walked away or purchased something I later regretted, never to return. Jack exercised kindness and consideration for individuals in abundance. After one outing to Mitchells to pick up some suits, blazers, and slacks, I received a package from Jack and his team containing a bottle of wine and a beautiful handwritten note. I continue to be a customer today.

So, what do soup vendors in Pompeii, Herbert and Stanley Marcus, Walt Disney, Ira Neimark, and Jack Mitchell all have in common? They all understood a great deal about the importance of delivering exceptional customer experiences, all long before Lou Carbone coined the term "customer experience" in 1994.

How will automation, machine learning, data lakes, master data, cloud computing, AI, and 5G impact customer experience? To get the answers, I reached out to some key consultants and executives at large technology service providers to get their perspective on where the market is and where it is headed. We will explore these answers in a later chapter.

KEY TAKEAWAYS

1. Customer experience has been around since early commerce began; we just didn't have a name for it.

    If history has taught us anything, it's the importance of customer experience. Those who focus on it have a better chance of not only surviving but thriving.

2. Research and history prove that even your most loyal customers may leave you if they experience a poor experience with your brand or company. This is more important than ever since customers now have a much larger platform to speak from, such as Yelp, Google, and other review sites.

3. At least in the retail stories I shared, all these founders and/or executives prioritized customer experience. This focus on experience helped create a competitive barrier and allowed them to charge a premium for their merchandise and services. As the PwC research highlighted, customers are willing to pay 16% more for luxury items when the experience is better.

    By exploring history, we can better appreciate why customer experience has become so important and review which strategies to replicate or avoid in our own businesses today.

chapter 2

The Cost of Not Paying Attention

In this chapter, I will take you through a handful of stories and cautionary tales detailing how big companies make big mistakes with customer experiences and end up in the "business graveyard." Following our acronym, dear reader, and starting with "**S**," you will learn that it is so important to step up and pay attention. As customers, this is becoming far too common: brands we have loyally supported for years, if not through generations of our family before us, are suddenly cheapened as the executives in charge move toward inexpensive, outsourced, mass production and save money by refashioning themselves as a no-frills experience.

Some corporations are becoming too big to care; from the lofty heights of NYSE success, the folks in charge need to remember the loyal customers who initially financed their greatness. The attitude almost feels like one of disdain.

"They'll keep buying no matter what, so let's squeeze more and more profit. Our customers won't mind and may not even notice."

Guess what? They *did* and *do* notice. It shouldn't feel like this. A customer should feel wanted and cared for. It won't be all horror stories, though. We will also touch on companies that did it right and continue to do it right to this day. Can you make any guesses as to which companies I will be referring to?

In 1994, Sears, a hugely successful chain of department stores that took over America and Canada in the 20th century, had 3,500 stores across North America. How many of you have fond memories of receiving the Sears catalog in the mail? A 500+ page extravaganza offering pretty much anything you can think of, including clothes, housewares, toys, electronics, and tools. For kids of the '80s and '90s, the winter edition was particularly well received, as pages with circles scrawled on them offered Santa some polite suggestions for the Christmas and Hanukkah list. And believe it or not, my grandfather even purchased his first home through the Sears catalog in the 1940s!

They were known for stocking and creating top brands, such as DieHard, Discover Card, Kenmore Appliances, and Craftsman. Their Craftsman tool brand offered high-quality, American-made tools, including lifetime guarantees with every product. Furthermore, they had employees that cared and were equipped with an impressive amount of knowledge on each product they sold. The customer experience was engaging and empathetic rather than purely transactional. When you shopped in one of their stores, you came away with the feeling that you were a valued customer, not just another means to their profit.

Fast-forward three decades, and Sears has only 23 of those 3,500 stores to their name. This fall-off was due to many things, including the rise of dot-com competitors and poor management decisions. But you could also argue that Sears was starting to drop the ball on great customer service and experience. They decided to chase fast profit and began to make their tools overseas in China. Not surprisingly, the quality was far below that of their original range. Lifelong customers who were happy to pay more for well-made goods felt cheated as the brand they trusted no longer represented the high-quality, made-in-America ethos they had invested in for years.

The business graveyard is full of companies that opted to cut costs while sacrificing customer experience and employee experience. Kodak is one such example. Established by George Eastman in the 1880s, they grew rapidly over the following 70 years. By the 1950s, Kodak controlled almost 70% of the US film market. They were elite. Right up to the 1990s, Kodak remained a dominant player in their market. They made their fortune from selling photographic films, which could be easily purchased from stores like Costco. While you have probably heard of the likes of Steve Jobs, Jeff Bezos, or Elon Musk, you may not have heard the name Steven Sasson. However, his contribution to modern technology was hugely influential and forms the basis of modern photography today. Sasson worked at Kodak, and in 1975, he built a prototype for the first digital camera. This was over a decade before competitors like Nikon, Cannon, and Sony brought their versions of this technology to the market.

Fast forward to the present day, and digital cameras are now the biggest seller amongst budding photographers and experts alike. The technology is even embedded in the mobile devices we carry 24/7. However, Kodak has lost most of their market share and now barely keeps afloat. So, what went wrong?

The potential success of digital cameras was obvious; they were far more cost-effective for the consumer in the long term and offered amazing advances in functionality. However, this posed a problem for Kodak. They made much of their profit from selling rolls of film, so they were reluctant to release the blueprint for their digital camera. They feared it would undermine the value of their original product, film. The management at Kodak only focused on the negatives of digital (its lofty size, slow processing, and poor resolution) without really digging into its potential and working to iron out the kinks. Set in their ways and afraid to rock the boat with traditional 35mm film, they decided upon a protectionist approach to their business, choosing to keep their digital design locked away in their vault. This shortsighted and fear-led decision eventually led Kodak to its fall from grace. On January 19, 2012, Kodak filed for bankruptcy. If Kodak had focused on the new potential that digital technology offered instead of clinging to their hold over traditional 35mm film rolls, they would still be at the forefront of modern-day photography. Hindsight is a wonderful thing, but it won't change the fortune of companies like Kodak. The reality is that Kodak could have focused on putting their customers' interests at the heart of what they did and avoided their free-fall into oblivion. The short-term pain of helping customers move from 35mm to digital might have been tough, but I am sure the reward would have not been bankruptcy.

The reward for providing a good customer experience is customer loyalty. However, hard-earned customer loyalty can disappear overnight if a company attempts to drastically shift its business model. In the early 2000s, Target decided they were going to re-imagine themselves as a "stack 'em high, sell 'em low" budget goods provider and compete head-to-head with Walmart. Walmart dominated the everyday low-price end of the market and were unfazed by the competition. Walmart said, "Come on in, the water's warm!" This wasn't misplaced confidence. Walmart knew their market, and Target was trounced. Target failed to recognize what their customers wanted—the details that made them unique (bright stores, friendly faces, and well-dressed, helpful employees). You'd go to Target because they offered more pizzazz than Walmart. (Okay, not high-end luxury. But just a little more style. Some might say trendy on a budget.) They stocked well-known brands and created private label brands in partnership with well-known designers. All of this was in an atmosphere that was less chaotic than the average Walmart (you've seen the YouTube videos on Black Friday when people swarm the store for $99 flat-screen TVs, right?). Customers didn't mind paying a bit more at Target because they knew the associates, quality, and overall experience would be better. At Walmart, you know exactly what you are getting. You're getting all substance, no style. You're getting the occasional very under-dressed customer and shirts for $9.99 that lasted a few weeks or months at best. It is a place for no-frills bargains to be sought. After a few short weeks, sales dropped following a massive drop-off in customer traffic. Target was forced into a sharp U-turn back into their previous market space. Customers simply said, "This is not what I signed up for. If I wanted minimal service and cheap goods, I'd have shopped at Walmart." I give Target a lot of credit for attempting something new. More importantly, I give them more credit for realizing the mistake and quickly getting back to the business they knew so well and customers loved them for.

The thing about Walmart is that they don't try to be anything other than "the cheapest in town." They can afford to cut corners and get away with it if their prices can't be beaten. Unlike Target, which runs its business in line with more conventional industry standards, Walmart's cheapness runs in its veins—they are the masters of cutting costs. I was unfortunate enough to experience this firsthand on a visit to Walmart HQ in Bentonville, Arkansas. I remember waiting in a room with 50 other people to meet with a Walmart buyer; it felt like a scene from the 1950s that was never remodeled rather than the HQ of a multi-billion-dollar corporation. We were all waiting to get the green light to be able to speak with their various "higher-ups" in rooms that led off from the cattle holding area. After 30 minutes of waiting, a bell rang. Everyone scurried into tiny rooms, but not before buying a cup of coffee for 25 cents. The whole experience left a bitter taste in your mouth and your fingertips burnt from the cheap and very thin paper cups. One thing was clear. Walmart was consistent with their business model; it was designed from the top offices down to the shop floor—lowest cost at any cost.

Once, a large soda distributor decided to open an office in Bentonville, Arkansas, since Walmart was one of their biggest customers. After they settled in, some execs at Walmart visited the soda distributor's offices. A far cry from their own humble abode, they were confronted with fancy couches, comfortable chairs, and top-of-the-range appliances; the coffee and soda was free too. Rather than complimenting their business allies on their smart environment, they responded by telling them, "Your furniture is too nice—return it." This wasn't a bout of unbridled jealousy; this was an opportunity for them to make more savings. "Sell all your fancy furniture, wall art, and then use the money you save to reduce the price of the product that we sell to our customers." They'd have had the soda distributor execs sitting on cardboard boxes if they could pass on a few cents of savings to their customers. The savings would be tiny and the culture change for the soda distributor massive, but Walmart lived by those principles and felt their suppliers should too.

There are now well over 300 suppliers that have their offices in Bentonville to serve Walmart. Although things have improved over the last 20 years, I assure you, none of the offices have nice furniture.

As far as Target, they continue to find ways to differentiate themselves from their largest competitors—Walmart and Amazon—both of which have far more to invest in acquisitions, marketing, and volume buying to keep prices low.

For example, in 2017, Target bought Shipt for $550 million to allow them to leverage their physical locations and offer same-day delivery in many markets—a relatively modest investment to help compete with Walmart and Amazon.

More recently, they leveraged their unique differentiator of having Starbucks in many of their stores. Now when you are ordering for pickup, you will see an option to add a Starbucks drink to go. *The Street's* Colette Bennett wrote:

> If the service is available in your area, once you place a drive-up order via the Target app and indicate that you're on your way to pick it up, the app will display a pop-up offering the option to add on a Starbucks order. When you arrive, the drinks and/or food items will be delivered to your car along with your Target order.[8]

---

8   Kline, Daniel. "Target's Bold Bet Helps it Keep Pace With Amazon, Walmart." The Street. Accessed August 6, 2023. https://www.the street.com/retailers/target-has-a-surprise-success-walmart-and -amazon-dont-offer.

What a great customer experience that is very difficult for Amazon and Walmart to replicate.

Finally, Target leveraged what they know best—creating iconic brands that customers love and can't find anywhere else but at Target.

Sometimes private label brands can be considered a less expensive option than your favorite national brands. That is not the case at Target. They pride themselves in creating unique, quality brands that are not only reasonable but high quality. Successes include "A New Day" women's apparel, "Made by Design" Housewares and luggage brand, and "Good & Gather," a line of ready-made pasta, meats, sauces and other prepacked foods. In a recent article on *Thestreet.com*, Rick Gomez, Executive Vice President and Chief Food and Beverage Officer for Target Corporation, pointed to the success of the company's Good & Gather when he wrote, "Value is top of mind, but we have to think about value more holistically than just price."[9]

More recently, we watched the NYC taxi industry crumble in front of our eyes.

At its peak in 2014, an NYC medallion that gave you the license to drive an iconic yellow car was selling for just over $1 million.[10] Now, let's consider the overall customer experience. Cabs were hard to flag down, especially on a rainy day. When you did hail a cab, it was not always that comfortable.

Although many drivers were friendly, you could not easily leave a rating on drivers that were not living up to the promise

9   Kline, "Target's Bold Bet Helps it Keep Pace With Amazon, Walmart."

10 Khafagy, Amir. "NYC Yellow Taxi Medallion Crisis, Explained." Documented NY. Accessed August 17, 2023. https://documentedny .com/2021/11/23/taxi-cab-medallion-explained/.

of being a good Yellow Cab driver. This customer experience was ripe for innovation.

Enter Uber and Lyft. Overnight, they completely changed the experience. You could easily hail a cab from your phone and watch the progress as your driver got closer. The pricing was competitive and, in many cases, less expensive. The drivers also took pride in their cars and how they looked inside and out since they were personally owned. If you had a great experience, you could easily tip and leave a review. If the experience was less than satisfactory, you could provide a lower rating and help other customers avoid the experience you went through.

Within a few years, the price of the medallion for a Yellow Cab went from just over a million to roughly $80,000 in 2021.[11] Could Yellow Cab have avoided this fate? A resounding yes. The industry became complacent, and they monopolized the market. If they had only taken the time to see the issues of their industry and how dissatisfied customers were with the overall experience. Uber and Lyft were early friction hunters! They saw lots of friction in the process and tackled it using technology and an entirely new approach. In an upcoming chapter, we will cover the importance of being a friction hunter. Let's agree that Yellow Cab ignored the customer experience and paid a hefty fee.

Another example of a business neglecting its customer experience and paying a high cost is JCPenney. JCPenney, founded in 1904, had made its name as a department store that offered coupons to customers looking for bargain buys. They were a great success for decades, establishing 2,053 locations by 1973. The store operated under a consistent model for over one hundred years, but all was to change in 2011 following the

---

11 Khafagy, "NYC Yellow Taxi Medallion Crisis, Explained."

appointment of Ron Johnson as their CEO. Johnson was hired after having success with two other massive brands, Target and Apple. Johnson wanted to transform the business, and instead of implementing a staged roll-out, he pulled out all stops to satisfy his "transformative vision." He took everything the customers knew about the coupon-driven chain and threw it in the trash. Johnson wanted to simply transplant the approach he used at Apple onto a completely different business model. He believed that customers would come to JCPenney because it was an interesting place to hang out and then wouldn't mind purchasing items at "everyday low prices." This was incredibly shortsighted, and unsurprisingly, this strategy backfired and blew up in his face. Johnson's method alienated their once loyal customer base who had become accustomed to heavily discounted items. By eliminating the thrill of bargain hunting, the new pricing strategy pushed away customers who felt they had been cheated. Johnson openly admitted that he had "disdain for JCPenney's traditional customer base."[12]

Johnson wasn't done, though. While shoppers were reacting poorly to his new policies, did he admit his error? Not likely. He doubled down on the customers, believing that they needed to be "educated" on how the new pricing strategy worked.[13] Unsurprisingly, this attitude failed to win over customers, and they went to rival department stores and online. After all, as the saying goes, "The customer is always right." JCPenney is now a shadow of its former self, with only 667 stores intact. They have

12 Duprey, Rich. "J.C. Penney Finally Remembers Who Its Customers Are." Finance.Yahoo. Accessed August 8, 2023. https://finance.yahoo .com/news/j-c-penney-finally-remembers-133600757.html.
13 Duprey, Rich. "J.C. Penney Finally Remembers Who Its Customers Are."

spent the last few years battling against bankruptcy.[14] The lack of empathy and customer care during Johnson's reign hammered the final nails in the coffin of JCPenney. His time as their CEO has been described as "one of the most aggressively unsuccessful tenures in retail history."[15]

While Kodak and JCPenney have struggled to rebuild their success, some companies have found themselves with one foot in the graveyard but managed to pivot and find their way out. IBM should have a sideline in ballet dancing for their history of notable pivots. Originally founded as the Computing, Tabulating & Recording Company (C-T-R) in 1911, the company officially became IBM in 1924. Back then, IBM was known for tabulating machines, punch cards, and other office supplies. In 1981, IBM realized that they needed to modernize their business and quickly moved into the personal PC market with the full support of their executive team. By the mid-1980s, IBM dominated the personal computer market, while Apple was just trying to hang on to the educational market. Unlike Kodak, they seized upon the opportunity to offer their customers more, instead of holding them back from modern advances. If IBM had opted to stay focused on the punch card and tabulating machine business, my guess is that anyone born after 1980 would have no clue who IBM was or that they even existed.

In 2005, they boldly decided to sell off the PC business that had allowed them to thrive. They instead focused on mainframes and consulting; this turned out to be another wise move for the company. And in 2021, IBM announced its third major pivot,

---

14 Chutchain, Maria. "J.C. Penney Rescue Deal Approved in Bankruptcy Court." Reuters. Accessed August 1, 2023. https://www .reuters.com/article/us-jc-penney-bankruptcy-idUSKBN27Q0FB#.
15 Tuttle, Brad. "J.C. Penney's Pricing Is Faker Than Ever" TIME. Accessed August 9, 2023. http://business.time.com/tag/ron-johnson/.

splitting its business consulting business from its technology business. In doing so, they created two of the world's largest brands—IBM and the newly-formed Kyndryl. All three of these moves were not only good for IBM but great for their customers and the overall experience of working with them. Although, it is perhaps worth pointing out that Apple, the company that once operated in their shadow, has eclipsed them in terms of revenue. I mention this because it is a little-known fact that the first smartphone was invented by none other than IBM in 1992—they peaked too soon, and it didn't take off.[16]

Much like IBM, many companies that are household names today looked very different in their early years. Netflix has become a huge player in film streaming and production, but it started off as a DVD movie supply and rental business founded by Californians Reed Hastings and Marc Randolph in 1997. DVDs had only been invented two years beforehand, and Netflix was the first to ask the question, "Is it possible to safely ship them direct to homes?"

After a few successful test runs, the answers came back with "yes!" They quickly moved forward and became an overnight success. Their whole concept was founded upon facilitating customer convenience. "Why go to Blockbuster when I can have movies shipped directly to my home for a reasonably priced monthly fee?" Blockbuster is now out of business; go figure. In 1998, Jeff Bezos (currently the 4th richest man in the world) offered the two founders roughly $14 million for the business, but they (wisely) turned him down. By the year 2000, with the dot-com boom underway, Randolph and Reed offered their

16 Heathman, Amelia. "The Smartphone Turns 25: Here Are the Five Major Milestones of the Device." Verdict. Accessed August 7, 2023. https://www.verdict.co.uk/smartphone-invented-25-years/.

business to Blockbuster for $50 million, but Blockbuster turned them down (not wise). Two years later, Netflix went public, and by 2004, they were generating roughly $500 million in sales. In 2007, they delivered their one-billionth film to a customer in Texas. Simply incredible.

Netflix owned the rental market. And, once again, they could have followed the same path as Kodak and just kept plodding away with their current offering, not paying attention to competitors and market trends. However, they were much braver and committed to being front-runners in film distribution. So, they invested in building a streaming service that they launched in 2007. The rest, as they say, is history. As of the date of writing this book, Netflix is the world's most subscribed streaming service, ahead of rivals Hulu, Amazon Prime, Disney Plus, and Apple TV. Crucially, when they shifted the direction of their business, they didn't lose sight of the customer experience. They offered the service to customers at no additional cost to help build the initial adoption. There have certainly been some bumps in the road for Netflix, and no one said leadership and amazing customer experience was easy. But Netflix has more than held its own.

Let's finish with three out-and-out success stories. First, there's GoDaddy, which is a domain registration and web hosting company that was founded in Phoenix, Arizona in 1997, just ahead of the boom in the online industry. GoDaddy's commitment to providing good customer service is relentless. When you call them for support, you will likely be left satisfied—in an ever more impatient world where offering solutions rather than creating more problems is worth its weight in gold. Out of roughly 60 conversations I have had with them, I was impressed with 59. I'm putting that one less satisfactory experience down as the exception that proves the rule—these guys have mastered customer experience and are profiting from steady growth as a result. Often, transactions and services managed online become stressful when things don't go to plan. Without face-to-face in-store contact, we often find ourselves floundering when looking for help. Realizing this, GoDaddy makes sure that they are easily contactable, offering every possible avenue of communication to their customers.

Whether you want to speak to a representative over the phone, video chat, chatbot, or email, they have it all covered. Many of the more successful start-ups have taken a similar approach to GoDaddy, offering a broad spectrum of options to the customer to ensure they can contact them in the most convenient and accessible way.

Other companies who prioritize profit over customer experience have shut down call centers or moved them overseas, seeing them as an unnecessary overhead. But how many times have you sat in front of your computer, pulling your hair out as you trawl through seemingly endless and irrelevant "common queries" on a company website, only then to resort to an AI assistant who still can't give you the answer you are looking for? It's the sort of experience that will leave a sour taste in the mouth of the customer and push them into the arms of competitors offering a better standard of service. Once again, cost-cutting can work out as an expensive business choice. The harder you make your customer's life and the longer you take to resolve their problems, the less likely you are to retain their business. While businesses grow and look to expand their customer base, they sometimes neglect the importance of retaining the loyal customers that made them successful in the first place.

Just as GoDaddy has great customer service through its multiple communication options, Apple has created a well-valued customer experience through in-store engagement. Just the other day, I had to take my daughter to get a new phone from the Apple Store. It was a Tuesday, and we showed up 15 minutes before the store even opened. There was a line eighteen people long (which is a measure of their popularity). People were willing to wait fifteen or so minutes in line because they were confident that once they were inside, their problems would be resolved with little effort and minimal stress.

Their formula for creating a great in-store environment is ensuring their employees are friendly, engaging, and (crucially) know what they are talking about. They aren't just salespeople, they are all experts in the products they sell. You can speak to one person and get the answer you need. No being passed around different departments, no glazed-over looks from people who don't know what you're talking about, and no reluctance to put in the extra effort. By the way, the rest of the shopping mall where this Apple Store was located was empty.

Steve Jobs created this simple and effective business model when he reunited with Apple in 1997. On returning to the company, Jobs whittled down their 48-product offering to just four. He didn't want Apple to be just any manufacturer and retailer; he wanted them to represent luxury and exclusivity.

Good is no longer sustainable.

You need to be great or step aside. Jobs decided he was going to make the most exceptional cell phone in the world. It would be the most beautiful to look at, made from premium materials, perform better than the market rivals, and host the best and most innovative apps available. Apple may operate in the tech industry, but really, this is just the way they facilitate their real focus—selling customer experiences.

Last but certainly not least, I had a chance to connect with Michael Roberto, a professor who teaches and conducts research on leadership and decision-making at Bryant University. In June of 2023, Professor Roberto and David L. Ager, Senior Fellow and Managing Director, Executive Education Harvard Business School, published a case study on their research on Tractor Supply Company, a company that has grown year after year since the mid '90s! I asked the professor why a traditional brick-and-mortar store like Tractor Supply has consistently done so well when other retail giants have fallen during the same period.

He stated that they are thriving even as many other brick-and-mortar retailers have collapsed for many reasons, including:

1. They invested in truly experiential retail. Customers not only get very knowledgeable assistance in-store about how to care for their animals and land, they also can use the self-wash station to wash their pets/animals, can get their animals vaccinated at in-store clinics, and can even trade animals and knowledge at the "chicken swaps" held periodically outside of the stores.

2. They have invested in creating community within their stores. Customers come to talk with one another. As they say, people love to talk about their animals almost as much, IF NOT MORE, than they love to talk about their kids! They also love to hire their customers because they already live the lifestyle that Tractor Supply is about.

3. They have used their digital presence to make buying online and picking up in-store seamless.

   They realized that this option is important for many of their rural customers. People want to browse the store but love the notion that they can guarantee that a key item they need is in stock before they head to the store (which might be some distance away).

4. They also use their mobile app to deliver important help and knowledge for their customers as they try to care for their animals.

5. Finally, they have this incredibly fun policy that allows people to bring pets into the store if they are leashed. Believe it or not, people have even brought horses into their stores!

So, I then asked Professor Roberto the question you are probably also wondering about. Does all that focus on customer experience impact the bottom line? Professor Roberto responded with a "YES!" Tractor Supply's revenues had grown every year since the early 1990s, and the company had been the 4th highest performing stock in the Standard & Poor's 500 Index since 2000. Comparable store sales growth was astronomical during the pandemic (over 20% in 2020 and over 15% in 2021) and still strong in 2022 (over 6%). Sales per square foot increased from $260 to $381 from 2015 to 2022. You can learn more about this incredible success story by reading the full case study on the Harvard Business School website—https://www.hbs.edu/faculty/Pages/item.aspx?num=64166

The failures and successes in this chapter remind us that customer experience can be defined within a brand and the customers that support it. Therefore, any changes to the brand identity must be taken with caution and follow modest steps. Customer experience is intertwined with customer expectations. If you fail to manage those expectations by treating your customers as incidental to profit, you'll learn the hard way that loyalty is eroded far quicker than it is built. This goes for the employees, too, and their employee experience. If they fail to match the values offered to your customers, the whole project will come apart at the seams. Even if the wisdom of executives around you suggests you need to reconsider your offering, remember that customers will tolerate familiarity far better than change. Change can be an important part of developing a business, but this mustn't be done at the cost of losing your business's identity. And, in some cases, this identity might include bringing their pets, including horses, into the store. If you are trying to scale up your business, don't forget your foundations—stick with what you know works. If Walmart started selling Rolex watches, we'd find ourselves with two brands that have deceived their customer base and will likely pay the ultimate price.

KEY TAKEAWAYS:

- Just because you were a success in the past and your clients loved you does not guarantee you success in the future. Avoid what Sears and Kodak either could not see or refused to react to.

- Know when to pivot. Markets, customer preferences, technology, and competition all change over time. You need to be ready to make moves or change markets completely. IBM and Netflix are masters of this. By using customer experience as a guidepost, you can help ensure that your business evolves over time to keep up with trends and market demands. GoDaddy is a perfect example of this. It is what has helped them stay on top of their market.

When done right and with sincere intention, this focus on customer and employee experience can be extremely profitable. Just ask Tractor Supply shareholders.

chapter 3

Hire a Team of Ruths

EMPLOY

In 1996, Google was two years away from its official launch; it was still a pipe dream being developed in a garage in California. Therefore, when I needed a nearby optician, I couldn't simply "Google search" and browse through the paid ads at the top of my screen. So, it wasn't any search optimization wizardry that led me to find Ruth, the owner of a store in New York City called 10/10 Optics; it was good, old-fashioned local convenience. The store was right around the corner from where I worked, just off Fifth Avenue. I wasn't lured in by flashy signs, newspaper promotions, or any other sales gimmick. I just chanced upon the store as it was what I needed, where I needed it. Flash forward 26 years, and I am now great friends with Ruth and a lifelong, loyal store patron. I must have now visited 10/10 Optics over 50 times, but the seed of this long-term relationship was planted at my very first visit.

This chapter is part one of Employ, the "**E**" in S.E.D.U.C.E. How can you attract and employ the best teams to create memorable customer experiences?

When I first walked into Ruth's store, I was immediately greeted by one of her sales associates. She offered to hang up my coat and then introduced me to Ruth. After a friendly greeting, Ruth asked me, "What brings you in today?"

I told her that I was looking for a pair of glasses that would make it easier for me to read my work.

She chuckled and smiled. "No, John," she said. "What style are you looking for?"

In hindsight, walking into an optician and telling the owner you are looking for glasses wasn't my smartest move; she had already made that wise assumption all by herself. Ruth's question had caught me unprepared. I hadn't given much thought to style. But, of course, if these glasses would be furnishing my face for the foreseeable future, I should probably get a pair I liked the look of. Trying to quickly conjure up a style reference, I replied, "Erm… something like Michael J. Fox's wireframes, perhaps?"

She took a moment before responding, staring intently into my eyes with the same obliging spirit that a mother has toward her confused child. "I'll take it from here," she said with a tilted head and a slightly cracked smile. After 15 minutes of trying on frames, she laid out three final pairs and gave them to me straight. "John, these are the frames you are going to choose from today."

I felt like I had my own personal stylist. I guess, in a way, I did.

"Option one is the safe option, a neutral style that is similar to the glasses you walked in with today. Option two is slightly more sophisticated. Option three is the game changer. And I can tell you now that you are leaning toward option one."

She was absolutely right. She was so good at her job that she could get the handle on a customer after only a short time in his or her presence.

"But…" she continued with delightful confidence, "… today, I'm going to sell you option three because it's the best option for you."

I stood and contemplated whether or not I was going to push back against the bold recommendation. Then, hesitantly, I put my faith in her vision for me (excuse the pun) and bought those "game-changer frames."

As I left the store, I was a little worried about my decision. However, within 30 seconds of my exit, I received a compliment. I thought to myself, "Wow, she's good. She's hired someone to stand outside her store and compliment people. Clever." It wasn't until my fifth compliment on my commute home that I realized that Ruth wasn't just a master salesperson, she was a genuine provider of exceptional customer service and great customer experience. After about two weeks, I was very comfortable with my new look. And I was feeling more self-confident than I had in a long time. Customer service is not simply about the product or service that you offer; in many ways, that's incidental. It's far more about how you make a person feel throughout the purchasing journey and after the transaction has been made. We need more Ruths; we need more people who truly care about providing exceptional service to their customers. While raw profit remains the single focus of many businesses, customers will continue to see brands enter the market, only to exit through the same revolving door they came in through. If you capture our attention, you must foster our interest and care for our needs. Ruth does this very well, which is why she has been around for so many years. It's also the reason why I take a six-hour round trip every time I fancy a new pair of frames. So, how do we go about finding more Ruths?

Just as I explained with Walmart, whose customer experience (or anti-experience) trickles down from the head office to its stores, the customer experience ethic of a business must be upheld consistently throughout all its departments. This can only be guaranteed by paying particular attention to the hiring process. It's important that each employee representing your business checks every box from your company's list of values. After all, you can have a beautiful store and brilliant amenities, but that will go to waste if the people presenting it are failing to convert this into an excellent customer experience. Therefore, we need to ask ourselves, "How do we ensure that our interview process is attuned to identifying the right people for the task at hand?" The hiring process should reflect everything and everyone in your company. Every link in the chain needs to be as robust as the next, from the CEO's office to the company cafeteria. For example, suppose your employees are having a bad experience at the company cafeteria. In that case, it's not enough to rely on great leadership because you're ignoring the importance of the staff serving the coffee and food. Every position needs to be hired under the premise that they should function with the same pride and dedication to the business as the CEO; without establishing company-wide respect for the business, the business won't be able to consistently deliver the customer experience they have planned from the top.

When the airline JetBlue first started, they had a unique approach to hiring flight attendants. They sought out people with the skills needed to deliver an exceptional customer experience and targeted former first responders. When they asked candidates questions about their work experience, such as, "Tell us how you have helped someone," they would be able to answer along the lines of, "Well, I pulled a woman out of a burning building once." JetBlue's philosophy was that if you were able to pull someone out of a burning building, attend to people who were seriously injured, and work well under the pressure of an emergency, they were confident that you were going to be more than capable of making sure people were safe, comfortable, and well-attended during a commercial flight. JetBlue is still ranked as a top airline when it comes to customer experience.[17]

Although they have had some growing pains over the years (some that I have experienced personally), they have kept intact their approach to hiring exceptional crew members to ensure an exceptional customer experience while flying 30,000+ feet above the earth.

JetBlue figured out their hiring strategy.

Unfortunately for customers, companies enjoying rapid expansion often decide to sacrifice the quality of the product or experience they offer in order to expand their business to meet the demands of a larger market share. Take Starbucks as an example. In 2005, it had roughly 9,000 stores (an impressive amount in itself). However, as of 2022, they had 34,317 stores worldwide. This is staggering growth in a relatively short period of time. But how can they be expected to maintain their reputation for high-quality roasts, expertly-trained baristas, and top customer service when they have expanded that rapidly? The infrastructure necessary to implement the high standard they could offer in 9,000 stores cannot be easily replicated in

---

17 J.D. Power. "Airline Demand-Supply Imbalance is Good for Revenue, Tough on Customer Experience, Says J.D. Power." Accessed August 26, 2023. https://www.jdpower.com/business /press-releases/2023-north-america-airline-satisfaction-study.

a business that now owns almost four times that number. The rapid growth caused some of the issues Starbucks faced with employee and customer experience in the 2020s. Many, including myself, would argue that leadership also caused some of the issues.

Thankfully for Starbucks shareholders, employees, and customers, Schultz returned as CEO of Starbucks in 2022 and committed to investing $1 billion (with a B) in customer and employee experience. Everything from employee apps to help create a better employee experience to higher pay and programs to support partners, including Master Roaster and Black Apron programs, are back.[18]

Just like JetBlue in their early years, Amazon has maintained high standards by investing in an expertly designed recruitment process. Early in the company's development, founder Jeff Bezos introduced people that he called "bar raisers."[19] These are skilled evaluators who are employed to interview job candidates. Bar raisers can veto any candidate, regardless of which department they are applying for. Bezos has said that implementing this role has helped Amazon weed out the "cultural misfits" and ensures they are only hiring the best-fits, as every interviewee has to be approved by a diverse range of interviewers.[20] Another thing that sets Amazon apart from its competitors is its outside-the-box approach to the internal organization. For example, they

---

18 Fast Casual. "Starbucks Investing $1B in Employees, Customer Experience." Accessed August 10, 2023. https://www.fastcasual.com /news/starbucks-investing-1b-in-employees-customer-experience/.

19 About Amazon. "What Is an Amazon Bar Raiser?" Accessed August 2, 2023. https://www.aboutamazon.com/news/workplace/amazon -bar-raiser.

20 Moss, Caroline. "Being One of Jeff Bezos' Designated 'Bar Raisers' Is like Having a Second Job You Don't Get Paid to Do." Business Insider. Accessed August 27, 2023. https://www.businessinsider.com /amazon-bar-raisers-2014-1.

have a policy called the "two-pizza rule" which dictates that if the attendees of a project team meeting can eat more than two pizzas amongst them, then there are too many people in attendance. The smaller the team meeting, the more efficient the decision-making is—so long as there are enough in attendance to represent a balance of ideas. So how does Amazon apply their "blue-sky-thinking" to customer experience?

Unless you live under a rock, you can see that Amazon is everywhere. You can walk down almost any street in America, and there is at least a 25% chance of seeing an Amazon delivery van drive by. Bezos and his team at Amazon have created the most efficient delivery service that the world has ever seen. Not only can we expect next-day delivery on many of the orders we make, but we can also expect this promise to be true for most deliveries. How is it that this triumph of customer experience has been created by one of the largest companies in the world? Well, the key to their success lies in their ability to scale their processes. They remain committed to delivering the best service possible, regardless of the size of their business. Their success has nothing to do with luck but rather from their appointment of talented people at every level of their operation.

Amazon isn't invincible. They may well need to improve their employees' working conditions if they want to retain the support of their millions of customers worldwide. As I have mentioned before, a successful customer experience is dependent on an equally successful employee experience. Since they put so much effort into employing the right people, they would do well to put as much effort into retaining them. For decades now, Amazon has fought off attempts by workers to set up labor unions following walkouts and protests against their working conditions. This suggests that Amazon's employee experience is nothing to be desired. Amazon has many complaints and lawsuits to their name, with claims that the company discriminates against gender and race and has failed to address sexual harassment in the workplace.[21] If the employee experience really is as bad as it sounds, before too long the customer experience will be affected too. Turbulence within the inner workings of an organization will always affect the output made available to customers.

From gloom to boom, let's talk about Google. Now one of the most recognized brands in the world, they are a major player in global tech innovation. Google's success is clear. They roughly occupy 93% of the global search market and are worth roughly $763 billion on the US stock exchange as of 2023.[22]

But how did Google get to this point? How did they scale so well? Their products alone aren't the secret to their success. Google officially launched in 1998 from a garage in Menlo Park, California, that belonged to the friend of founders Larry Page and Sergey Brin. The company grew quickly over the next few years, and in 1999, they moved their offices to Palo Alto, California. Their first major investment came from Andy Bechtolsheim, who invested $100,000 into the start-up. As the company grew, so did its need for an exceptional workforce to push the company forward. In order to streamline their recruitment process, they devised "humanized" interview questions that focused on the character and values of their candidates. I have firsthand experience of this, as I was asked to provide a reference for a Google interviewee. Instead of asking me to list the candidate's generic strengths and weaknesses, they asked

---

21 Greene, Jay. "Five Women Sue Amazon for Race and Gender Discrimination." Independent. Accessed August 1, 2023. https://www.independent.co.uk/news/world/americas/amazon-women-gender-discrimination-b1850722.html.

22 Oberlo. "US Search Engine Market Share in 2023." Accessed August 30, 2023. https://www.oberlo.com/statistics/us-search-engine-market-share.

me to tell them about a time where the candidate had "been sympathetic to others in the firm" and a time when they had "done something unexpected." Their non-conventional approach is mirrored in the company's internal practices too. For example, they offer employees periods of "innovation time off," where employees are encouraged to spend 20% of their time at work on projects that interest them. Allowing their workers creative freedom has paid off, as Google apps such as Gmail, Google News, and AdSense have all been created by employees during this innovation time. Therefore, Google is a great example of what happens when you focus on employee experience. This creates a foundation of success where the true mission of the company can flourish. The customer experience directly benefits from this as the service is delivered with pride and from a place of creative freedom, providing the consumer with the best that tech has to offer.

Since it is always important to practice what you preach, I have developed my own best practices for delivering effective employee recruitment. When I hire my employees, I look for the qualities of a Scout. I look for people who are "trustworthy, loyal, helpful, friendly, courteous, kind, obedient, cheerful, thrifty, brave, clean, and reverent," which are characteristics that make up the "Scout Law." I would rather hire someone who possesses most of these characteristics and practically zero knowledge than someone who has amassed a wealth of knowledge and none of these noble character traits. After all, I can teach people the practical/technical side of the job, but I cannot teach someone characteristics they need to have adopted from a young age.

KEY TAKEAWAYS:

- If a company wants to provide the best possible customer and employee experience, then its first investment needs to employ a world-class team, and that starts with hiring a world-class Chief Human Resource Officer (CHRO). A customer-focused company needs a CHRO that occupies a central leadership position, rather than an old-fashioned business model that pushes HR into the periphery.

- Ensure that the principles of your company are embodied within everyone that represents it. Use your employee interview process to find candidates who are best placed to promote and enhance your organization's values. Hire a "team of Ruths"—individuals who are enthusiastic, passionate, meticulous, and customer-focused regardless of their role within the company.

- The biggest challenge to employee-company-customer harmony will come if you attempt to scale. My advice is not to jump into massive growth like it is an overnight ambition. Carefully plot your expansion so that every part of your company's processes that have made it a success thus far can be preserved in the final version. Get big. That's fine and desirable, but don't get so big so fast that you lose your moral grounding. That is the kind of boom that will go bust.

chapter 4

The Autonomy of Employees and Their Experience

EMPLOY

Employ is so important it requires two chapters. Once you have a strategy in place and a team to implement it, you'll need to ensure these two components connect. With this in mind, the second part of "**E**" for Employ is empowering them to deliver exceptional experiences.

In early 2000, I found myself sprinting through JFK airport to catch my flight to Las Vegas. I dodged and weaved between small children with my case bouncing behind me. I was sure I was leaving a trail of sweat in my path like a snail on speed. As I approached my gate like a marathon runner ready to hurl himself over the line, I was confronted with the discombobulating fact that my plane was three hours delayed. There I was, racing like a madman, when I could have been sipping coffee and reading the *New York Times* for all it mattered. Standing there with my hands on my head and sweat dripping down my face and back, I felt deflated. "This means I won't get to Vegas until three in the morning Eastern Standard Time. I'm going to be exhausted," I sighed.

Hunched over in an ergonomically disastrous faux leather seat, I counted the hundreds of minutes in limbo. A first-world problem, I admit. Eventually, we boarded our plane, and a few cramped hours later (sorry, I should stop complaining, but my general state of being fed-up is relevant), I arrived. After a long taxi ride through Las Vegas traffic (it must be experienced to be believed at three a.m.), I made it to my hotel. Big relief. Walking into the lobby, I remember being greeted with warm smiles. I felt that they could sense I needed some TLC.

"Welcome to New York!" said the receptionist.

In the spirit of getting through the worst of a long day, I joked, "I'm sorry. I'm a little confused. I just came from New York. You're telling me I'm now back in New York? How is this possible?"

We shared a laugh, two strangers enjoying a human connection.

"One second, sir. I'll be right back," she said as she disappeared into a back room. She emerged not two minutes later.

"Since you traveled from New York and found yourself back in New York, I guess you're home! To make amends for your confusion, we've upgraded you to our largest suite."

Of course, the New York New York hotel in Las Vegas had nothing to make amends for. They were just being kind to a tired, stressed, and ultimately very grateful guest. After such an exhausting day, the prospect of sleeping in a cozy bed felt like heaven, let alone being upgraded to a 1,300-square-foot room with a view! Unlike the airline I had traveled with, the hotel impressed me.

They didn't need to upgrade me; it was purely an act of generosity. As a customer, this made for an unforgettable experience. And guess what? As a man who values good customer experiences, I make it a point to stay in the New York New York Hotel every time I'm in Las Vegas. Since I was only booked in until 10 a.m. the next morning and the suite's next guests weren't due until later that day, the upgrade only cost the hotel the time of some late morning housekeeping. The effort was very much appreciated—so they have earned themselves a shout-out in my book!

The point is that it wasn't about the amount of extra effort they were willing to give; it was about their focus on the customer experience and the fact that the staff didn't have to go through five pieces of red tape to make a routine stay become a special one. The front desk staff had been trusted with the power to make a business decision, which reflects very well on their brand. They didn't have to seek out a top-down edict in order to make the day of this exhausted guest considerably better. I slept very soundly that night. It is incredibly important that employees are empowered to make good decisions because a brand will suffer if its values remain purely theoretical due to bureaucracy. I always frown a little when someone says, "I will have to talk to my manager" or "I'm not authorized to make that decision." Of course, it's not the employees' fault. In fact, they are often victims of poor procedure too, and they'll bear the brunt of angry customers due to a policy that is above their pay grade. The New York New York hotel had good procedures in place. They allowed their staff to use an opportunity to add value to their guest experience and create lifelong customer loyalty from yours truly. So, the lesson here is that as well as training your employees, you must also empower them. Otherwise, good intentions are left at the front desk and never materialize into great customer experience opportunities.

When I was Vice President of Sales and Edible for Business at Edible Arrangements, a franchise with over 1,200 locations globally (at the time 2014–2017), I remember attending a regional franchisee-run event in Massachusetts. During the event, I was approached by a gentleman that was probably in his early fifties.

He approached and said, "Hi, my name is Bob, and I am a delivery person for Edible Arrangements. They call me Bob, the singing and dancing delivery man."

I asked him why they called him the "singing and dancing delivery man."

He said, "When I am delivering a special arrangement for a birthday, for example, I will sing Happy Birthday and even wear a special birthday hat that has candles on it. For example, just last week, I delivered a special Edible Arrangement fruit bouquet to a woman celebrating her 80th birthday. I rang the bell, and when she answered the door, I said 'Happy birthday!' Then I said, 'Now I have to split,' and I did the actual split there on her porch and handed her the bouquet of fruit."

I said, "Wow, what was her reaction?"

"She smiled and laughed a bit when I did the split."

Bob walked away, and a few minutes later, the owner of one of the franchised locations in Massachusetts walked up and said, "I see you spoke with Bob, one of my delivery people."

I said, "Yes, wow! What energy and passion he has for what he does. He must really love his job."

"Yes, he does. By the way, Bob did not tell you the full story. A few hours after Bob delivered the arrangement, the woman who ordered the arrangement called and asked to speak with the owner. Sometimes that can mean there was a problem, but in this case, she wanted to share a story about her mom, who the delivery went to. She explained that her mom had lost her son unexpectedly two weeks ago, and she had not stopped crying and was not eating. She said, 'Your delivery man had no idea, and he just did what he does best and sang a birthday song for my mom and even did the split. For the first time in two weeks, my mom smiled and even laughed for a second because of Bob. She even ate several pieces of the fruit. I want to thank you and your delivery person for helping my mom smile, just for a moment, during this very tough time. THANK YOU.'"

I asked the owner if she trains her team to sing and do the splits.

She said, "No, but I give them the freedom to put their own spin on the delivery, and Bob's spin is extra special."

This is another powerful example of how empowering your employees can truly impact your business. Bob and Edible Arrangements can't change the fact that the customer lost their brother and a mom lost her son, but they can bring a small glimpse of happiness, even for just a few moments.

Employee autonomy facilitates good customer service and enables staff members at every level to support their company in providing excellent customer experiences. When I was the CEO of Kenosia, a software company I co-founded in the late '90s, we had a policy of a mandatory two-week sabbatical. In practice, this meant that you were awarded two weeks of additional sabbatical during your third year with us. This upped the annual vacation from three to five weeks. We encouraged our employees to invest this additional time off to go somewhere they hadn't been before to take in some new experiences. Often, they would come back to work with a load of stories to share—sometimes offering us valuable market research about customer experience.

However, our main goal was to reward our employees for their loyal service while offering them a better working experience. As a result of this attitude, we had a brilliant employee retention rate. We rarely lost anyone and regularly grew. Perks aside, another part of our employee success was our culture of autonomy for the employees. We trusted the people we hired to make good business decisions. Since we were much smaller than some of our market competitors, we couldn't compete on salary alone. Offering employees responsibility and a degree of creative freedom, therefore, gave us the distinguishing feature we needed. Most of our employees could have gotten jobs at bigger firms where they would have been making more money, so we had to create an inviting culture that differentiated us by offering (non-monetary) added value to our working experience.

Here is another great example of a firm that truly focuses on the employee. I had the opportunity to sit down with Sudhir Singh, CEO of Coforge, at an event to celebrate their achievement of reaching $1 billion in annual revenue. During our conversation, I asked Sudhir what some of the contributing factors were to reaching that impressive milestone. He explained that employee retention was crucial and a characteristic that helped them stand out above their competitors. The proof is in the pudding. Coforge has a 14.1% attrition rate, which is extremely low compared to many industries that have attrition as high as 40%+.[23]

One example of how Coforge went above and beyond to support their employees was how they handled the Covid-19

---

23 Hansen, Jefferson. "Understanding Employee Turnover Rates (And How to Improve Them)" Awardco.com. Accessed October 20,2023. https://www.award.co/blog/employee-turnover-rates#:~:text= Turnover%20rate%20by%20industry%3A&text=Information %3A%2045%25,Education%20and%20health%3A%2045%25.

crisis. In the early days of the pandemic, Coforge opened its headquarters campus in New Delhi, India, to not just employees but their families as well. If you could not find a way to get to their campus, Coforge would send a vehicle to get you. Sometimes it might have been a truck, but they arrived. At the headquarters, Coforge recruited doctors from not just India but from around the world to help their employees and their families. Parents, grandparents, and, of course, children. They also invested in purchasing as many oxygen containers as possible to help with the efforts. Coforge was not the only firm to go above and beyond for their employees during Covid, but it is certainly an example of why employees stay and thrive at the company.

Now let me tell you what bad employee autonomy looks like. In 2008, after leaving Kenosia, I was looking for a senior role with a large research firm where I could leverage my industry experience and relationships. Over 10 years, I built up a large Rolodex of who's who in the Consumer Packaged Industry. A senior vice president at L'Oreal who was a customer of mine at Kenosia and now a personal friend made an introduction to one of the two largest research firms at the time for the retail/consumer packaged goods industry. I had an initial phone screening interview with the person I would be reporting to if I was hired. We immediately hit it off. Within a day or two, I had an invitation to fly out to Chicago for an in-person meeting with the president of the company, HR, and a few other key executives that I would be working with if hired. I took a seven a.m. flight out of LaGuardia, and everything went smoothly. The day was starting off strong! I called my soon-to-be boss to let him know I landed and would arrive at the office a bit early if he wanted to grab a cup of coffee before a long day of interviews. He answered and sounded surprised.

"They didn't call you and let you know?"

"Know what?" I said, a pit growing in my stomach.

"I gave notice yesterday and am heading to the airport now. Your interviews are still on, but the schedule has been changed a bit as you would be reporting directly to the head of US sales."

"Ah, okay," I said.

"Good luck, John. You are going to do great, and I am sure our paths will cross again."

Not the end of the world but certainly a shift in how smoothly the day was going so far. I arrived at the office in downtown Chicago about an hour early. I let them know I had arrived, and HR said they would send someone down to greet me shortly. Three hours later, a just-out-of-college HR associate walked down and introduced himself. He apologized for the delay and said things were getting shifted in my interview schedule because of some internal "fire drills." Instead of lunch with a few of the executives, he would be taking me out for an early lunch.

A bit confused, concerned, and frankly disappointed, we walked a few blocks to a very nice restaurant. The college grad ordered the lobster salad (the most expensive lunch item), I guess because the business was paying. We had small talk for an hour. Frankly, red flags were going up about the company culture of the business and if this was going to be a fit, but I thought to myself, "I flew all the way to Chicago, so let me play this out."

We arrived back at the office at close to one p.m., and he asked me to wait in a small office with no windows while he rounded up the people I would be meeting. Nearly an hour later, he retrieved me from my holding cell and walked me over to the head of HR.

Her first words were, "I am really busy, but I'm glad we could meet for a few minutes."

No apology for the long wait leading up to the first interview. I was made to feel like I was an inconvenience to her. We chatted for about thirty minutes, and then she said she needed to get to a few things and would walk me back to the small office where I would wait for my next interview.

No, not the holding cell!

Thirty minutes later, I was walked over to the head of US sales. This was a 25-year veteran of the business, and he didn't waste any time.

"Listen, John, our sales cycles can take years. I need someone that is willing to build relationships and, over time, secure business."

I wanted to respond with, "Yes. This is usually how it's done, and it's why I was flown out to Chicago to meet with you."

But I didn't. Instead, I simply walked him through my experience and industry relationships. Then I asked some questions about his biggest challenges, the current team, and areas where he thought they had an advantage.

After an early morning flight, hours of waiting, a wasted lunch opportunity, and a strange interview with the head of HR, we were getting somewhere. An hour later, I can honestly say the interview with the head of US sales went well. Yet, the waiting still wasn't over. I had been told to wait another thirty minutes to meet with the president, but alas, there was a fire drill. It was all for naught. The odyssey was finally over, and I was on my way back to the airport to fly home.

I was not impressed with the experience, and it shed light on what the business would be like to work for. By the way, interviews are not just for the employers; they are also for the prospective employees to measure you and your team. This experience received a solid D minus. I wanted to leave room in case I experienced something worse. Twenty years later, this team still had the record. The SVP and friend from L'Oreal that helped make the introduction called the next day to ask me about the interview. I was professional but did share my experience including that my soon-to-be boss gave notice earlier in the week, the odd lunch with someone from HR, the holding room, the two interesting interviews I did have, and the three or four interviews that never transpired. He was shocked and apologized. I thanked him for the introduction and assured him there was nothing to apologize for.

The next morning, I received a call from the head of HR that I met while in Chicago. Remember the one that was too busy to meet me? She apologized for the poor experience and said they would like to fly me out again for a full day of interviews. I kindly declined and said my time was valuable, but if they wanted to fly in some executives to meet with me in their Norwalk, CT office, which was a forty-minute drive, I would make an effort. She suggested I pick a date that worked for me. The following week I had the opportunity to meet several senior leaders from their company, and it went well. If this was the first round, I might have been excited, but first impressions leave a lasting mark. Although the make-up sessions were great, my decision had been made. I politely declined the offer, and it was one of the best decisions I have ever made.

The anatomy of your employee experience starts when you are interviewing prospective employees. If your culture is chaotic with lots of fire drills, cancellations, and always letting the urgent get in the way of the important, you are going to hire more of the same rather than hiring talent that can help shape your business for the future.

Onboarding is a key aspect of business management that you

cannot afford to overlook. Sure, bean bags, ping-pong tables, and free sushi for lunch may be inviting, but the real game-changer is understanding the importance of technology. In the next two to three years, 85% of the workforce will be made up of millennials—the first generation to expect well-integrated technology when they walk into an office. They will want to have multiple screens at their desk and the flexibility to work from tablets and phones with a seamless transition between devices, not to mention remote work options. Underestimate the importance of technology in a contemporary workplace, and you'll see your intake quickly disperse to better-resourced rivals. Without a decent technological infrastructure in place, employees will feel isolated and cut off from the business as a whole. Technology is the most effective way to maximize effective intercommunications. This will generate a culture where ideas are shared rather than hoarded or left unheard, and there you have a model for employee autonomy.

A successful company won't have a mission statement that reads, "Make as much money as humanly possible, profit at all costs." This mantra is simply unsustainable as it neglects the need to nurture and retain employees and encourage them to promote good customer experiences. Without happy employees or satisfied customers, your profit will be zero. For example, at Information Services Group, Inc. (ISG), our values include "trust, integrity, and work-life balance," to name a few. These values are not just words on the website. Mike Connors, the founder, chairman, and CEO of ISG, lives by them. He is a role model for his direct reports, who in turn are role models for their reports. By the way, "trust, integrity, and work-life balance" are not brand differentiators for ISG; many firms have these or similar terms in their value statements. The differentiators are the actions of your employees day in and day out with their peers and the firm's clients. These values represent things that we all believe in and endeavor to incorporate within our business practice.

As you think about incorporating representable values and morals into your mission statement, you need to consider how your employees are impacted by the employee experience. There is a danger of overvaluing either the employee or the customer at the expense of the other. This is something I call the Five/Two Scenario. Five stars from one end (customer) and two stars from the other (employee) or vice versa. If you have a five-star rating from your customers but are only getting two-star ratings internally, you're not going to last unless you act to even this out.

Amazon is an example of a company that is in danger of prioritizing customer convenience over employee working conditions and is dealing with a string of lawsuits because of this. Eventually, a poor employee rating will catch up with the business's output and seep through to the customer experience; as employees become dissatisfied, they will unconsciously lower their standards and commitment to company guidelines, as it is human nature to reject the rules when we are dissatisfied by the governance enforcing them. To make sure you keep the balance in check, I recommend conducting customer experience and employee experience surveys on a monthly or quarterly basis. Customer experience starts with the employee experience; the two should be treated equally.

An example of a poor employee experience comes from a friend of mine who recently accepted a job as an account manager for a company she was excited to work for. She had turned down another offer with a lower salary, which seemed like an obvious decision at the time. Unfortunately, her first day only dampened the excitement she'd felt after being offered the position; she was not only unimpressed but shocked at her treatment. Upon arriving, there was no one to greet her. After eventually finding someone to speak to, that person didn't know who she was or that they were expecting a new employee. She couldn't have felt less welcome. After finally being recognized by someone in the building, she was shown to her desk and given a laptop with the expectation that she would go straight to work. However, in order to log into the computer, she was asked to download a security app onto her personal device, which she felt uncomfortable doing. For the next two days, she sat at her desk for eight hours straight with no work assigned to her and not a soul to talk to. It was as if they didn't know she was there. Unsurprisingly, after seven days, she left the job. When she gave them her frank feedback, they didn't even seem surprised. That's the sign of a company with no soul or backbone. I know, without seeing it, that "employee experience" isn't featured in their mission statement or company guidelines. And if it does, it's only words on a page. The sad fact is this is a company earning $20 million a year in revenue. They have the resources to make the onboarding process welcoming and supportive of their new hires but, instead, deliver an experience that is memorable for all the wrong reasons. My friend lasted a week—I can say with some confidence that this will represent their overall employee retention rate. After leaving that job, she returned to the other position she'd been offered, accepting a little less pay and slightly worse hours. Thankfully, after only two weeks, she absolutely loved it. They greeted her at the door and sent her a welcoming letter the day before she started. Her coworkers are kind and supportive, the work is engaging, and there is a culture of valuing employees—definitely worth sacrificing a little salary for.

Developing a culture within a business must be both top-down and bottom-up. After deciding which talent to hire, a business must ensure they can match the new hires with the values and morals they wish to promote. This is done through the hiring process. A great example is when I went to an interview at Bristol Technology; one of the interviews was with three engineers and involved problem-solving. Although I was applying for a sales position, they still wanted me to have the problem-solving skills that everyone else on the team possessed. It was a remarkable experience. One of the problems was along the lines of "A bird is traveling at fifty miles an hour east and a train is traveling at sixty miles an hour west. There are fifty miles in between them. How long is it going to take before the two cross paths?" I managed to give an answer, and they rewarded me with even harder questions. We laughed and joked a little, and I did my best to answer them accurately. They nurtured me into the right answer when I got to the hardest questions. I walked away from the interview contemplating how their interview process would affect the team culture within the work environment. I also went home and bought a book on brain teasers. If I did get another round of interviews, I was going to be ready. A week later, I got the job, so I soon found out. When they are interviewing engineers, they expect them to figure out the puzzles because they need people that can solve problems. However, when they interviewed me for a sales position, they were less interested in me getting the right answers and more interested in my curiosity and whether I got frustrated. The same interview could be used to determine different desirable skill sets. By using a test to gauge the reaction of potential employees, they have successfully built a culture of people that are curious, accepting, and nurturing to others.

I could feel it with all the people I was working with. This company's employee retention was excellent, well over 90%. I was part of that organization for many years, and I don't think I can remember more than a few people that left during my time. In fact, it's the business that Kenosia, the company I mentioned earlier, was born from. Brilliantly done.

So how does technology fit into employee experience? I sat down with Melanie de Vigan–Biver, Vice President, Head of Portfolio and Pre-Sales for Atos Digital Workplace and People Experience at Atos, an $11 billion euro global IT and services provider based in Bezons, France. Melanie is focused on creating solutions to deliver exceptional employee experiences for Atos clients. Melanie's work focuses on three areas:

1. Bringing together disparate employee data sets.

2. Moving toward a more predictive approach to employee support and experiences.

3. Creating an omnichannel for employees, so regardless of the device or where they leave off, they can continue to work and/or receive support.

Atos is a true friction hunter. More on friction hunting in a few chapters.

When I asked Melanie to explain this further during our conversation, she said, "Understanding each employee is so critical to delivering an exceptional experience.

"If you understand that one employee prefers to receive support through chat and another via phone with a live person, you can cut down on delays, inconvenience, and, frankly, frustration. We need to be careful to only extract the employee information that is necessary to deliver the right experience. We must also help our clients bring disparate data sets together to create a more holistic approach and experience."

While having dinner with the CEO and founder of Microland, Pradeep Kar, a 34-year-old service provider based in India, he was excited to share their internal app for employees. Everything from checking your productivity, emails, pay stubs, and 401K could be accessed through this simple app.

Want to write a note directly to the CEO?

Done!

Send out a quick survey to employees?

No problem!

Maybe you just want to share a personal announcement that you are super proud of?

Easy as a click.

Pradeep said, "We have been working on this internally for over seven years, and our employees love it. We are now ready to share this solution with our clients so they can build a stronger employee experience."

The company Ensono takes a unique approach. At every one of their team and executive meetings, they set a place around the table for a teddy bear named Ernesto. As strange as this may first seem, the bear represents the customer voice and provides a constant reminder for attendees where the business's focus should be. This empowers employees in those meetings, regardless of their title or years of experience, to say, "Let's ask Ernesto." Of course, the bear can't talk (maybe in the future with ChatGPT), but by asking the bear, employees are empowered to push back on ideas that might harm customers. It's very empowering, and it works. Ensono customers love the company, and their employees feel like they are involved in that process.

When I asked Paola Doebel, SVP and Managing Director of Ensono North America, about their approach and how they manage to keep their clients front and center in all their decision-making, she replied, "You have to love your clients. At Ensono, we don't think of our clients as transactional. We think about them as clients for life." She explained, "That means you really have to understand them; you have to set up an account structure that supports them individually. Beyond that, you need to think about how you treat the client contractually instead of just the human element of interaction. We created Ensono Flex® to provide clients the flexibility to move workloads across Ensono managed platforms with no penalty."

As we closed out our interview, Paola left me with this thought that I just love. "We're not always after the fast nickel; we're okay with the slow dime."

As you think about your business and your customers, are you okay with the slow dime?

From all my conversations in the industry, this trend of building stronger employee experiences is a key component to customer experience and overall success. It is wonderful to see firms like Microland, Atos, and others developing solutions to create those environments for their customers and employees.

From the employee back to the customer. The next chapter looks at the experience you receive before you have even become a customer.

KEY TAKEAWAYS:

- Ensure your employees are empowered; they need the authority to make decisions that will positively impact customer experience. You need to put guardrails on this, as everyone's interpretation is different. Taking the friction out of the process of approvals for small things can create huge positive impacts, which are critical.

- Ensure you and your team take the interview process seriously. Far too often, interviews are seen as "getting in the way" of daily work when that time is actually some of the most valuable you and your team can spend. Future hires are the lifeblood of ensuring your company culture and values stay intact. First impressions truly matter.

- Once you make the hire, the real work begins with developing an exceptional onboarding process. This will ensure the new talent is engaged with the business and understands in depth the company culture and values. A great first week also reassures the new hire that they made the right choice. One study found that companies with an effective onboarding plan retained 91% of their first-year hires.[24]

---

24 Doerr, Randi Renee. "What Should a New Employee Do for the First Week?" Exact Hire. Accessed August 2, 2023. https://www .exacthire.com/hiring-process/what-should-a-new-employee-do -for-the-first-week/.

chapter 5

Acquiring and Retaining Customers

DESIGN

We naturally think of the customer experience from the perspective of a customer. But the experience you offer should start before you have people queuing up to spend their money. Therefore, we move to the "**D**" in S. E. **D**. U. C. E.—Design experience for retention and acquisition.

I recently met with the Chief Revenue Officer for a multi-billion-dollar service provider, and she shared a story I will never forget. Her team was working on a large technology transformation deal that was worth roughly $100 million dollars for a Canadian bank looking to upgrade its entire system. We're talking user interface system upgrades, cost optimization, workplace upgrades, and the complete works. They were competing against two other large, world-class service providers worth over a billion dollars each and boasting global client outreach. This meant that they found themselves in a battle of wits trying to beat everyone else and come out on top. Each of the service providers was asked to submit a written request for proposal (RFP) document, which is a significant undertaking to produce. A few weeks later, her two competitors submitted their documents. Each was beautifully bound on high-quality, parchment-like paper with exceptional presentation. While the content within would be the main determinator of success, style can elevate substance when the competition is so fierce. She knew her team needed to find a way to stand out and connect with the bank. So instead of just submitting a strong, well-written, and competitively priced RFP response, beautifully bound like everyone else had, she instructed her team to build and send a dollhouse modeled to look like the bank's logo, which was a house. Each room in the dollhouse presented a separate section of the RFP. Perhaps this sounds like a gimmick? The concept offered far more significance. The CRO had clearly done her homework on the bank. This bank is incredibly committed to putting Canadians in homes, a mission statement on which their whole business model is based. The logo of the bank being a house reinforced that. By taking the time to research the bank's core morals, her company was able to demonstrate their commitment to the client's vision, demonstrating that they not only understood their technical needs but also the reasoning behind it. They ended up winning the deal. This wasn't because of the price they pitched, nor was it because they built an attractive dollhouse. They won the deal because the bank recognized that this service provider understood their business model, which offered them an edge over their competitors who were solely focused on flexing their technical skills. They were able to find a creative way that connected with the bank and acknowledged their mission statement. Impressive. They provided a connection experience with the bank before they had even become a customer of theirs.

Regardless of the type of business you run (whether you're a café, clothing store, or specialty bulk food store and coffee roasting house like the one my wife and I own in Newtown, CT), the mission of connecting with customers should begin before a single product is sold. It should begin when they are still only *potential* customers you are hoping to win over. In order to be a success in your local community, you should try to engage with the community that you are hoping to serve. Investing in local homeless shelters and food banks or sponsoring local school events shows you care about the community you operate in. They are then more likely to buy your coffee, clothing, or services. When all is said and done, most coffee shops use decent beans and top-notch barista equipment. A customer is much more likely to remember you if they see you as an integrated part of their community. Show you care about the customer before they have invested in you; this is the best way to build a sustainable and healthy business. If your community activity is newsworthy, you'll get free publicity from word of mouth as long as you continue to show that you care. Rather than just making a one-off gesture, you should have yourself a loyal customer base that grows over time. We all ask our friends for recommendations. Where did you get your computer fixed? Do you know where I can buy a secondhand car? Which café do you recommend in the area? Whatever the question, let the answer be your company because it is celebrated as a loyal, local servant.

After my daughter graduated from high school, we visited five universities, all of which had offered her academic scholarships.

When we visited the last of the five on our list, the students were seated in one auditorium and the parents and guardians in another large room. The president of the university came down to speak to the students and then immediately came over to speak with the rest of us. This was essentially a pre-sale meeting, as no student had offered their written acceptance yet. The president's talk gave us all a great impression of the student experience that they offered. The other universities were happy to show us around and provide information, but this wasn't delivered by their top representative. For the president of the fifth university to take time to invest in the pre-sale process demonstrated their commitment to the students, even before they had agreed to hand over their parents' hard-earned cash. The university was a real fit for my daughter, but this extra investment by the school helped win us over. This demonstrates the importance of being present, involved, and committed to potential customers to ensure that they become future customers rather than a lost opportunity. People like commitment, and people love to feel special.

Great experience wins deals. A few years ago, I heard a story about another technology service provider competing for a large contract with one of the market-leading diagnostic companies in the US. Since the company has locations all over the US, the head of sales leading the deal provided every person on her team with locations in their local community. Therefore, when they came to the meeting to present for the first time, they had their own informed perception of the customer experience the company was offering. As a result, her team was able to share personal experiences about how their technology solution would enhance the overall customer and employee experience. Her team ended up winning the deal. Certainly, the competition also had exceptional solutions, but her team had a unique perspective coming into the deal because they took the time to do their own research beforehand. That perspective gave them a competitive advantage. Not just because their ideas were more on point, but also because the diagnostic company could see how vested this team was in truly understanding them as a company. Do first impressions matter? Research from ISG-led engagements says "YES." Paul Reynolds, Chief Research Officer and Partner at ISG Research, found when a service provider's first impression is as expected, their chance of winning the deal is 70%. When your first impression is less than expected, your chances of winning the deal is zero.

For smaller local businesses, first impressions can have a huge impact. Take Ruth, for example. As a direct result of my positive recommendations over the past 25 years and counting, roughly 100 people have visited her and bought new frames. She's had people traveling from California, Chicago, New Jersey, and Connecticut to visit her store. Hence, an exceptional customer experience is itself great marketing for customers still waiting in the wings.

While there are fantastic and creative ways that companies and businesses have connected with their soon-to-be customers, there are also ways that have not worked out and ways that should be avoided. Here's a good example: a manufacturer from the Midwest was holding individual meetings with their service providers in their local offices. The meetings were conducted by their CIO, who was a woman. One service provider sent eight men to represent their company, all of whom were directors. This was a red flag for the CIO, who questioned the company's policy on diversity, equality, and inclusion, as well as the importance of this opportunity to the service provider because they did not include a senior level executive. Needless to say, they failed to secure any contracts with other service providers providing a more balanced, diverse, and senior team. The provider missed the one-to-one moment opportunity.

One-to-One Moment

To help illustrate this, let's use the brand Tide, a washing detergent created by Procter & Gamble roughly 75 years ago. This is now a household name, representing 15% of the global household detergent market. That's the kind of success that won't come out in the wash (sorry!). When Tide was founded in 1946, their marketing (like other consumer brands at the time) consisted of "general ads" plastered across the United States. I like to call this type of advertising "one to millions"—meaning one ad in Connecticut was the same as one found in Southern California—one ad was therefore used to attract millions. A few years ago, I created a concept I call the "Evolution of One." As an example, in the late 1940s and early 1950s, Tide was being marketed to the masses as a cleaning product that could provide you with "the cleanest clean under the sun." This generalized sales pitch used hyperbolic claims to capture the attention of as many stained-clothed-consumers as possible but offered very little consideration of the consumer themselves. As Tide's popularity expanded across the United States, Procter & Gamble chose to create more specified and personal marketing campaigns that were able to speak to consumers on a deeper level. In the 1970s, Procter & Gamble was airing Tide commercials that showed regular people being given the option between a box of Tide or two times as much of the leading competitor's brand. Everyone went with Tide, of course, but it gave consumers who watched the commercial a point of relationship. The ad also made existing customers feel validated in their decision to use Tide. This represents a much more specified "one to many" personalized way of marketing. As we moved closer and closer to the millennium, technology rapidly progressed. So did the way in which Tide and other brands marketed their products. Brands began to take advantage of email communication and made state-by-state and city-by-city campaigns. In my "Evolution of One" conception, this is considered "One to Few."

As ad campaigns started to get more tailored to individuals, they became more potent, and companies were able to see exponential growth as a result of their marketing. Nowadays, we have even moved on from the "One to Few" technique, with "One to One" marketing leading the way. This includes Google, Facebook, and Instagram ads—hyper-specified ads that are so in tune with the target user that it's almost frightening. How many times have you seen an online ad and then questioned whether your house is bugged or cameras are watching you?

The next stage in the "Evolution of One" is the "One to One Moment." With this, marketing is no longer solely preoccupied with one-to-one engagement but also in capturing a particular moment that represents the target consumer (much like the bank's dollhouse mentioned earlier in this chapter). This goes further than merely addressing customers individually, as it personalizes content based on a better understanding of that individual at that moment. This makes them feel not only pitched to but involved.

Debraj Bhattacharya, Senior Director, Industry Solutions and Sales, Retail and CPG at HCL Tech explained the ++ after Customer in their Customer 360 ++ model: "So, we are moving from hyperpersonalization to what we call a segment of one, which is each consumer DNA would need to get mapped with the offerings of a brand. We call this Customer 360 ++."

According to Bhattacharya, generative AI is one key piece to the puzzle of creating these segments of one. Although not there yet, they are very close.

Arnob Bhattacharya (not related to Debraj but works at the same company) is the Application Modernization and Innovation Leader for Google cloud ecosystem at HCL. "The first plus in Customer 360++ is the customer and their preferences. The second plus is the AI-driven layer." HCL Tech is currently working with a large exercise clothing retailer to enhance the omnichannel experience with their "guest" customers. So, now a guest can be shopping online, move to an in-store experience, and then buy through an app or in-store seamlessly. "We want to remove the 'friction' from the shopping experience," Debraj Bhattacharya said.

Arnob Bhattacharya explained how he invited his daughter to take part in a user research study:

> I actually had my 17-year-old daughter take part
> in our user research and experience study that was
> related to dolls. We wanted to find out what is it that
> this toy means to children and very interestingly, she
> said, "It needs to be memorable."

Bhattacharya's daughter nailed the magic word. Regardless of customer or employee experience, it needs to be "memorable" and for all the right reasons. Customer 360++ is a glimpse at what we can expect in the future with regards to a true segment of one experience. This is what I call "one to one moment" experiences. Regardless of the nomenclature, we can agree with Arnob Bhattacharya's daughter—the experience needs to be memorable.

Take the diagnostic center story as an example of a "One to One Moment." The team selling could have just created a "One to One" experience by sharing a standard presentation about the firms' capabilities, as well as identifying the areas they thought could be improved. However, their approach was creating a "One to One Moment" experience for their perspective client. Instead, the deal team became part of the customer experience offering a richer presentation of specific solutions. If you want to engage with your customer, creating experiences like this will give you a much higher probability of success than impersonalized or "one to many" marketing strategies.

To ensure you stay balanced, your goal is not to just gain customers but to also retain them. Companies that put all their energy into gaining new customers, at the expense of existing ones, will find themselves walking in circles. You often see energy companies, credit card companies, gyms, and banks offering promotions to new customers. This is all good and well, unless you fail to recognize the loyalty of those already paying for your service. Existing customers will resent having to pay more or get less than new customers, given that they are the ones who have invested already. As we explore ways to create incredible first impressions with potential new customers or clients, let's not forget about the ongoing work that needs to be done to retain them. Reynolds also shared a study done by ISG Research where thousands of large tech deals around the world were studied. What they found was that more than 60% of the time the incumbent loses all or part of the deal at renewal. These tend to be $50M+ deals, so losing half or all the deal can be a substantial hit. Focus on creating amazing first impressions, and then ensure you create a plan for ongoing impressions to keep them for life.

Today's computer algorithms are designed to create content

that retains your attention over prolonged periods of time. TikTok is a prime example (beware the doom scroll!). Retention is key, but how is this done? Well, the seed is planted before any selling takes place. Every customer you approach in the pre-sales stage represents a make-or-break opportunity. They are still making up their minds whether they like you, your business, or your product. It's like being a stand-up comic—the first ten seconds is where your audience will decide whether they find you funny; a poor start will dictate their willingness to engage with you going forward. It really is that quick—so first impressions count, folks. Human beings love to make snap judgments, as it is our primal instinct to seek out whether something is safe or valuable to us. In a business context, something as simple as a local ad will determine if the consumer pursues an interest or brushes aside their interest forevermore. Ads that strike a heartstring or tickle a funny bone will capture an interest. Those that fail to engage an emotional response will not. It is this initial experience, prior to the tailored customer experience, that will bring you success. You could have the best product or service in the world but that's of no use to you if no one is willing to try it.

My wife and I own a specialty bulk food and coffee roasting store in Newtown, Connecticut, called BD Provisions. A while back I was in the store when a woman approached me and said that it was her first time visiting us. We gave her our little tour and told her exactly what we do. As we were walking around the store chatting, I pointed out that we roast our own coffee. She mentioned she loved a good cup of coffee. After perusing our aisles, she said that she would think about coming back and thanked us for our help. As she walked out of the store and onto the sidewalk, I ran out the door with a half-pound of ground coffee in my hand and gave it to her.

"You had mentioned that you like coffee, so I wanted to give you a little to take home with you."

As a result, a vague "I may come back" turned into a loyal customer from that moment on. All for the price of half a pound of coffee. She has been a loyal customer of ours for years. That was a pre-sale, our "One to One Moment" experience, that turned a maybe into a resounding yes!

Ask yourself this: what are you doing to create an experience *before* someone becomes a customer? Have you considered everything? What does the outside of your building look like? How have you made the entrance welcoming or enticing? Are your customers greeted by a receptionist? When someone calls your business, do you answer the phone or does it go directly to voicemail or a call center?

For a great example of how impactful a quick response can be, try calling GoDaddy support. They certainly have chat options, but if you want to speak with a live agent, they connect you within minutes. And the person answering is not only helpful but incredibly knowledgeable about everything GoDaddy has to offer. Seven out of ten times I call their support line, I end up purchasing additional features or services. And I do it with a smile and a thank you.

I mentioned the purchase of my Volvo a few chapters ago and promised to get back to it. In 2018, my wife and I needed a new car. We are not big car people—no Porsche or Mercedes is required. We tend to get more excited about spending money on travel. So, when someone suggested a Volvo, we said, "That's a bit outside our range." Then they said that there was a new model, the XC40, that had just come out. It was a smaller version of their very popular XC90 and within our price range. The best part was my friend said that we could pick up the car at the Volvo factory in Gothenburg, Sweden for no additional cost. In fact, Volvo would pay for two airline tickets in upper class, two nights in a hotel, and a wonderful dinner out while in Sweden. I did mention that my wife and I love to travel, right? This was too good to be true, and we needed to learn more. The next week, we headed to a local Volvo dealer in Stamford, Connecticut. We took the XC40 for a test drive and loved it. When the salesperson gave us the final price, I thought that was the perfect time to mention that we wanted to pick up the car in Sweden. I was just waiting to hear about all the restrictions and complications that make it impossible. Nope. He simply said, "When do you want to go?"

Eight weeks later, my wife Cynthia, our two kids, and I were off to Sweden to pick up our new Volvo (we paid for our kids' tickets, and they sat in economy—sorry, kids). On arrival, we were greeted by a driver in a Volvo (of course) and dropped off at our beautiful hotel. That night, we enjoyed a wonderful dinner compliments of Volvo. So far, WOW. The next morning, we were once again picked up in a Volvo and brought to the factory to pick up our car. Prior to receiving the car, they took us on a tour of their car museum where we learned all about Volvo and what they are most passionate about. Can you guess? Safety! We learned about Nils Bohlin, the Volvo employee that invented the three-point seatbelt in 1959 that we all use today, no matter what car you are driving. Volvo had a patent for the three-point seatbelt, but they opted to share it with the world so all drivers and passengers in all cars could be safer.[25]

---

25 Volvo Buses. "The Three-Point Seat Belt – an Innovation That Saved over 1 Million Lives." Accessed August 16, 2023. https://www .volvobuses.com/en/news/2019/jul/the-three-point-seat-belt-an -innovation-that-saved-over-1-million-lives.html.

Volvo is so committed to what I call their superpower—"safety"—that they sacrificed short-term gains to ensure that customers and prospective customers knew what they were passionate about. Guess what? It worked. Cynthia and I knew Volvo was known for safety, but this tour sealed the deal for lifetime customer status, and we had not even seen our new car yet. After a nice lunch at the Volvo factory, the big reveal happened. The factory door opened, and there was Cynthia's new XC40. A beautiful Amazon Blue with black interior—just what we ordered. They gave us a full tour of the car, and then we were off to explore Sweden in our new Volvo for five days. It was a trip none of us will forget, and we look forward to doing it again when we buy our next Volvo. We dropped the car back off at the factory so they could ship it home. Then, of course, we were driven to the airport in—you guessed it—a Volvo! We then spent five days in Stockholm before traveling home. I share this story because the experience before, during, and after becoming a customer was incredible. What is your brand's superpower?

A brand that truly understands "One-to-One Moments" better than most is Chewy. While at a dinner party at a friend's house, I noticed they had a few small portraits of their three pets—two dogs and a cat. I commented on the pet portraits, and she said she received them as a surprise gift from Chewy a few months ago. For those non-pet owners or individuals not familiar with Chewy, they are an online pet food and pet supply company. Our friend told us that she had been buying her pet food for a few years from Chewy. Then one day, out of the blue, two portraits of her dogs showed up with a note thanking her for being a customer. A true one-to-one moment for my friend. So, I asked about the cat portrait. When our friend had called Chewy to thank them, she mentioned her cat. Low and behold, a few weeks later, a portrait of her cat arrived in the mail. Chewy has artists on staff to create these portraits for their customers. This is not only a great customer experience to help build retention, but a spectacular way to drive customer acquisition. Imagine how many people our friend has shared this story with. Dozens if not hundreds of friends and family members alike. Do you think any of them became Chewy customers? I would put my money on "YES." This isn't the only way Chewy creates memorable experiences. When a customer's pet passes and they call to cancel their pet food subscription, they refund the customer for the last order and ask them to donate the remaining food to an animal shelter. On top of that, they send a sympathy card and flowers. Not only incredibly thoughtful, but my guess is if that former customer gets another cat or dog, they will order their pet food through Chewy. You might not create personalized pet portraits for your customers. But what would be appropriate to surprise and delight customers to not only retain them but have them become your biggest champions for acquiring new customers?

As a final thought, you shouldn't prioritize new acquisitions or repeat business. Both are equally important and require continued maintenance. Once you have secured a new customer, you need to match or exceed the experience they received before they were a customer. A lot of businesses have separate pre-sales and account management teams. This is a flawed model because this creates a disconnect between the pre-sales and ongoing customer experiences. My recommendation would be to combine or connect these teams, so they become jointly accountable for net growth, in terms of securing new customers and retaining existing ones.

KEY TAKEAWAYS:

- Make an inventory of all the things that people could experience prior to becoming a customer of yours. Are you happy with the current journey or do some areas need improvement?

- Create Key Performance Indicators that incentivize both acquisition and retention. Alignment of the acquisition team and the management team is the best way to deliver this.

- A good customer experience is essential for the most cost-effective form of marketing available—good old-fashioned word of mouth.

chapter 6

The Friction Hunter

UNCOVER

When designing your customer experience, you need to look at all your processes. Ask yourself, "How can I make this better for the customer?" Here we will look at the "**U**" of S.E.D.**U**.C.E.— Uncover friction and resolve.

Walking down almost any street in America during the '80s and '90s, you were bound to see a Blockbuster store sign. It was the most popular home video service during this period, as anyone born before the millennium will know. Despite their market dominance, they were in an industry that was on the cusp of a dramatic reinvention, as technology was evolving at a rapid rate. Unfortunately, they were either blind to this or stubbornly resistant to the impending change. Blockbuster provided convenience. But, today, the prospect of having to get into your car, drive to a store, and hope to get the movie you want would be considered inconvenient. They already had to adapt from VHS to DVD, but they weren't nearly as prepared for the next stage of home entertainment. Who remembers having to rewind the VHS tape back to the beginning before returning it to avoid incurring a penalty fee? DVDs removed this obligation; however, scratched discs would cause the movie to freeze and jump as it played—yet this was the height of modern technology in Blockbuster's heyday.

Nowadays, this kind of tech looks like a hoop and stick next to streaming. While Blockbuster was set in their ways, market competitors seized the opportunity to carve out their fortunes by offering more and more convenience to customers. Netflix founders Reed Hastings and Mark Randolph devised a business model which focused on cutting out the inconvenience; they acted as a lubricant within an industry where time was the biggest source of friction. As I mentioned in chapter two, Netflix allowed customers to order their movies online, from the comfort of their office or living room, and receive the title a couple of days later by mail. On top of that, there were no fees, and you could keep the DVDs as long as you wanted. When you were done with them, you simply popped them in the mail using a prepaid envelope they arrived with. A stress-free experience. Of course, this was only the first stage of evolution, as gradually movie streaming services made the direct-to-your-door experience the new inconvenience. So, while Blockbuster was dragging its heels, Netflix was adapting fast.

Although Netflix is now number one, they weren't the first out the gate. They had a battle of their own to contend with. It was a rival American subscription service, Hulu, that came up with the streaming initiative. Overnight, Hulu stole the lion's share of the market right under Netflix's noses. At this crucial junction when DVDs were being replaced by streaming, Netflix had six million monthly subscribers, while Hulu was gaining tens of millions in a matter of months. Over the next few years, Netflix fully transitioned into a direct competitor of Hulu, overtaking them for top spot. Meanwhile, Blockbuster is no more.

Every part of Netflix is designed to offer their subscribers the best possible experience. Whether it be the accessibility of their platform, their ability to adapt to better technology, or the exclusives they routinely offer their millions of viewers, they put their customers first and have come out on top as a result. Before they became a household name, Netflix offered to partner with Blockbuster. They believed their innovation combined with Blockbuster's reputation would guarantee them a monopoly. Blockbuster was stubborn and laughed off the offer from the (then) tiny company; they failed to consider the future needs of their customer base and consigned themselves to the business graveyard.

Before 1999, if you went to a Disney theme park on a hot Saturday in June, you knew you had to be prepared for hours of waiting in line. Disney recognized this drawback and came up with a solution—the FastPass. The Disney FastPass was available to guests of the Disney Hotel. It allowed them to skip long lines and join smaller queues that were exclusive to pass holders. On its launch, the concept was a success. It has now been replicated by pretty much every large amusement park worldwide. Disney was able to smooth some friction and profit at the same time, as park guests were happier and able to spend more time shopping in the park stores rather than waiting in long lines.

Many of the world's biggest companies are formed off the back of pre-existing friction within the industry they have entered. As mentioned earlier, take Uber, for example. They took the friction out of hailing a cab, providing a more convenient experience to both driver and passenger. Now, virtually any privately owned car can become a cab. Drivers no longer need to drive around aimlessly on a slow night, hoping to catch wandering pedestrians. They can now sit back and wait for the customer to come to them. Likewise, the customer doesn't have to worry about finding an available taxi on the street. They can simply tap their coordinates into their mobile and have a driver arrive at their location in minutes. A frictionless experience is a good customer experience. New technology is completely revolutionizing and replacing old industry practices. So being ahead of the curve when it comes to customer convenience is a winning formula for any business.

Korean beauty store, Innisfree, invented a frictionless shopping experience by implementing a system of colored baskets. Customers who require in-store assistance are asked to take green baskets, while those who are happy to shop independently are prompted to take red ones.

Starbucks implemented an even more frictionless experience. They allow customers to preorder and pay for their drink on an app before collecting it from a designated pickup location in their shop. No need to interact with anyone—perfect for shy coffee drinkers or those in a rush. Customers can come into the store and leave with a coffee in hand without having to rummage in their purses or speak to a soul.

Plenty of innovation is now focused on creating the frictionless experience for both customers and employees, but how does a business go about developing new systems? One idea is having corporate employees spend time on the retail floor (if you are a retailer) or driving in a truck (if you are like UPS). A friend of mine that worked at the UPS headquarters in Atlanta in the early 2000s said that he would spend a day each year working at a delivery center or even on a truck. This was predominantly done to assist during peak seasons like the holidays, but it also gave corporate employees an opportunity to see what their teams in the field went through on a daily basis. As you think about your business, how can you ensure your team understands the ins and outs of the operation? Another friend that was an executive responsible for customer care at Walgreens said that he too spent a day working in the store each year. It was also to assist during busy seasons, but it gave him an opportunity to see policies they implemented at HQ in action. For example, it's easy to say, "Let's put up new displays each week"—at least until you realize the complexity and compliance issues you have in store.

UPS is constantly innovating. And whether these friction-hunting ideas came from executives working on the trucks or the drivers themselves, I love them.

UPS deliveries can be impacted by so many factors each day including weather, traffic, volume, and delivery locations. To help create a more predictable route experience, UPS created ORION (On-road Integrated Optimization and Navigation):

> Its advanced algorithms create optimal routes for delivery drivers from the data supplied by customers, drivers, and the vehicles and can alter the routes on the fly based on changing weather conditions or accidents. Ultimately, it will look at the deliveries that still need to be completed and continue to optimize the routes. The cost and time savings and emission reduction based on this optimization alone is extraordinary—UPS expects to reduce delivery miles by 100 million.[26]

26 Marr, Bernard. "The Brilliant Ways UPS Uses Artificial Intelligence, Machine Learning and Big Data." Forbes. Accessed August 12, 2023. https://www.forbes.com/sites/bernardmarr/2018/06/15/the-brilliant -ways-ups-uses-artificial-intelligence-machine-learning-and-big-data.

Another great innovation was designing their navigation software to avoid left-hand turns. They found it reduces time and fuel consumption and improves safety.

> As a result, the company claims it uses 10m gallons less fuel, emits 20,000 tons less carbon dioxide, and delivers 350,000 more packages every year. The efficiency of planning routes with its navigation software this way has even helped the firm cut the number of trucks it uses by 1,100, bringing down the company's total distance traveled by 28.5 million miles.[27]

I was not able to determine if these were direct outcomes from executives spending a day in the field, but no question, ensuring your team is connected to the decisions they make can have a huge positive impact on the overall experience.

When using outside technology and service providers, it's important that they are constantly bringing innovation to the table. And, at the same time, you are eagerly giving them that opportunity.

Ensono has found a unique way to encourage their clients to imagine the art of the possible by incorporating an innovation fund into their agreements.

According to Bryan Doerr, EVP of Product and Technology at Ensono, they have created an innovation fund with their profits to help clients engage them more formally in assessments and larger scale enhancements.

> We've created an environment where our clients are encouraged to explore forward-looking ideas and not

---

27 Kendall, Graham. "Why UPS Drivers Don't Turn Left and You Probably Shouldn't Either." GE. Accessed August 5, 2023. https://www.ge.com/news/reports/ups-drivers-dont-turn-left-probably-shouldnt-either.

feel locked in and frankly stuck. We not only help clients think about transformational enhancements, but we're also positioning for quarter-to-quarter general enhancement of the business. Enhancements could be driving out cost to free up funds for innovation, improving customer or employee experience, and/or security to prevent the next big issue.

Need further proof how important friction hunting is? Estes is the largest privately held freight transportation company in North America with over 8,500 trucks, 34,000 trailers, and a network of 270+ terminals to service clients. At a recent event, I had the chance to hear Todd Florence, the CIO of Estes, talk about their business. He explained their IT vision: to "make shipping frictionless for our employees and our customers."

This vision is so powerful. When I caught up with Todd later at the event, he said that "employees were mentioned first because if you have highly effective and happy employees, it will have a positive impact on the customer experience."

Todd also created an SVP of Digital Innovation to ensure there was someone sitting between the business and IT. I believe every company should have this senior position in place. No different than Walgreens and UPS, Estes's IT members are required to engage hands-on for a day each quarter to ensure they understand what Estes businesspeople are dealing with and help reduce or eliminate friction.

Outside of ensuring your technology partners are bringing innovation, be sure you and your team are also seeking out friction and opportunities. Whether you own a coffee shop, quick serve restaurant, or trucking company—go into your business and embrace the full customer experience. Sip the coffee, use the drive-through, drive the trucks, and visit the warehouse.

Whatever it may be, rid yourself of your corporate blinders. No skipping to the front of the line; you need to experience the wait that the customer has before being served their coffee. If it's taking too long or the coffee isn't hot when you go in for that first sip—time to go back to the drawing board and improve your system's efficiencies. If trucks are taking too long to load, there's friction—fix it.

Often, companies get lost in the efficiency of cutting costs. For example, a company may decide they can save a small fortune by introducing an automated call service. On the face of it, this may cut their costs significantly. But if it creates added friction for customers, the initial savings made will be eaten up by lost profits in the long run. If a customer has a problem with an order, the first thing they want to do is speak to a living, breathing human being. Generative AI may be the answer to many inefficiencies; however, direct human interaction needs to be at the heart of the customer experience (or at least the option needs to be available). People can apply their common sense to a problem and resolve it with minimal fuss. AI can only respond to a selection of anticipated questions, and it will require far more input from the customer before the problem is resolved. (Once again, I am sure Google, Microsoft, ChatGPT, AWS, and Tesla are working on it.) To deliver good customer service responses, you need to work with the knowledge you already have. What are the most common queries? For example, a lot of online customers will forget their password. So, having a system that directs customers to an immediate solution to this problem, even before they have reached an advisor, would be very prudent indeed. If a customer can problem-solve while on hold, this will free up the lines for customers with more complicated or unusual inquiries; win-win! Look at the numbers and use automated responses to cater to the masses, while allowing other voices to be heard directly and without unnecessary delay.

A seamless customer experience is a competitive experience— which is necessary when you don't hold a monopoly in your market. Therefore, local and federal government services are some of the most frustrating to deal with. You can be on hold with government agencies for hours because they have no competition and therefore no incentive to invest in the technologies that create a frictionless experience (to be fair, this could also be due to lack of budget). Next time you find yourself wasting your day trying to deal with taxes, getting a new license, or whatever it may be, take account of your frustrations and make sure you offer the opposite experience to your customers. Unlike government agencies, you'll have competitors ready and waiting to poach your business should your standards slip an inch. We saw this with Yellow Cabs in chapter two, who suffered at the hands of private-sector adaptability, with their popularity decimated by the far more flexible offering of Uber.

Much like radiation, friction in a business has a half-life. It's never zero—there is always an opportunity for change and improvement. Blockbuster chose to ignore their lifeline, and we know how that ended. So, make sure you respond to any friction that comes your way ahead of time. That's not to say you should be overly reactionary; sometimes technology needs further development before it should be adopted. Plenty of businesses fail because they invest too quickly on trendy or underdeveloped technology. Take the Sinclair C5 electric car, which was developed in the 1980s by British inventor, Sir Clive Sinclair. The project was ambitious but failed because the technology, while laudable, was not yet ready for mass market production. Forty years later, thanks to years of additional research, Elon Musk has made billions from electric cars. So, strike a balance. If the technology offers the potential of genuinely improving customer experience in a fundamental way, keep a close eye on developments. Don't be caught off guard by innovative start-ups (like Blockbuster was by Netflix or Kodak by digital photos).

While you can try to create the perfect customer experience straight from its conception in your business HQ, there will always be an element of trial and error. Not every seemingly good idea will be as well received as intended. As far as customer loyalty is concerned, it isn't the "thought that counts." It's important to be flexible and tentative when implementing new elements to a customer experience to prevent customers being driven away before you have time to make a sharp policy U-turn on an unpopular policy. Coca-Cola and their "New Coke" recipe is one such example. This beverage flop that was released in 1985 was quickly reversed with the original recipe being reintroduced almost immediately. It still remains popular today. Fun fact, "New Coke" was rebranded as Coke II, and it was finally discontinued in 2022.[28]

Don't just wait for stuff to hit the fan. Be proactive—become a friction hunter. Friction hunters look for potential bumps in the road, big or small, that may get in the way of optimal customer experience. Customers should never be treated like guinea pigs. The friction hunter's job is to analyze the circle of customer experience and look for potential potholes in the road that threaten to derail customers who are traveling through that experience. The circle begins with the very first customer experience, whether that's the first they hear from a company or the first time they step foot in a store.

---

28 Wikipedia. "New Coke." Accessed August 9, 2023. https://en .wikipedia.org/wiki/New_Coke.

First impressions are a big deal. Don't waste any opportunity to impress. Second chances are often few and far between in the hypercompetitive world of commerce. After a sale is made, the next experience a customer faces is the return experience—you caught their attention first time around and they are back for more—time to turn a returning customer into a fan. Never be under the impression that a second-time visitor is already a loyal customer, as the second visit can still be the last if the experience does not match or exceed the first. The name of the game here is consistency, which is the only legitimate route to loyalty. Once you have perfected and succeeded in creating a consistent experience, you should be rewarded with trust. The next step in the cycle is referral from friends of the satisfied customers, including social media posts and or reviews. When you lose one customer, you also lose their sphere of influence since they won't be making any recommendations in your direction. Those who have a great experience will recommend a friend and start the customer satisfaction circle again. However, this new customer will still have to be convinced their first time. If you are able to turn new customers into repeat customers and references, you will have the dynamics in place for a steadily growing business. The goal is to foster your own ecosystem, an ever-expanding circle of experience that will continue to expand so long as the experience remains consistent and in line with the company's values and vision.

KEY TAKEAWAYS:

- Friction hunting is like radiation. It has a half-life, so you never reach zero. You and your team need to consistently challenge the current process in search of ways to reduce friction moving forward. Technology will be one of the biggest influencers of this moving forward. Think about Blockbuster and Netflix.

- There is huge value to having your executives step into the shoes of your employees at least once a year. Many large brands find this practice invaluable, as they consistently find ways of reducing friction for not only customers, but employees as well.

- While looking to reduce friction, be sure you are not just chasing a trend that will come and go. There is a balance. Think about Sir Clive Sinclair and the electric car.

chapter 7

Interpretation

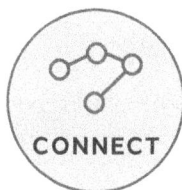

It is all good and well having excellent customer service embedded in the heart of your organization, but this serves little purpose unless the intentions behind those values are understood by customer and employee alike. Here we look at the "**C**" of S.E.D.U.**C**.E.—Connect the dots between intention and expectations.

A few years ago, my wife, our two kids, and I went on a trip through Ireland for ten lovely days. We drove around the country in a rental car. At various points on our journey, we came across a road sign with a symbol depicting an old-fashioned camera, the type you might see in films set in the 1920s.

"Great!" I thought. "They are pointing out scenic spots for tourists to stop and take a few pictures. How very accommodating the Irish seem to be."

However, some of the scenic views were a little underwhelming to say the least, which left us a little confused. Some of the signs pointed to castles and rolling hills, while others were simply residential areas—just private property with a few cows and dense tree coverings. Either the Irish were particularly proud of their cows or something didn't quite add up. Eight days into our visit and after ten less-than-scenic camera stops in a row, I decided to ask a local what this was all about.

"You know your scenic view signs? They are a bit hit and miss. Some of the stops offer gorgeous scenery, where others offer nothing to admire at all?"

A wide grin immediately appeared across the man's face. "Fella, those aren't scenic spots. Those signs are to warn you of speed traps ahead."

We could only laugh! But this made me think. Sometimes we misinterpret things presented to us so they appear completely different from the purpose intended. As hard as you try to make your message clear and accessible, you can never guarantee how it will be interpreted.

When I was the VP of customer service at Edible Arrangements (a company that specializes in the supply and delivery of fruit bouquets), we had a Texas-based furniture store, Gallery Furniture, contact us. They asked whether we were able to deliver "a lot" of arrangements to their customers on a month-to-month basis. After the initial inquiry, we began to consider how we could best facilitate their needs and offer them the best possible experience through the local franchised location closest to the furniture store. Then it suddenly struck us, what exactly is "a lot"? Would 25 be a lot, or perhaps 50 or even 100—we simply didn't know how to interpret the request. So, we downed tools, put our plans to one side, and went back to the client.

"And roughly how many arrangements did you have in mind?"

You can only imagine our faces when "500 ought to do it" was their reply.

"Wow, that is a LOT!"

So, as it turned out, speculating between 25 and 100 was way off. If we had run with that assumption, we would have fallen at the first hurdle. The furniture company wanted 400–500 arrangements a month to gift to their best customers. With such a high-volume order required on a regular basis, we needed to come up with a whole new model of operations in order to manage. Had we not asked for clarification and ended up misinterpreting the instructions, we would have run out of time to prepare our process. We would have lost the client along with hundreds of thousands of dollars a year. Lesson learned.

You have to make sure that your employees are all singing from the same hymn sheet and understanding the morals and objectives that your company stands by. Take Stew Leonard's supermarkets, for example. They have a large, engraved granite stone outside every one of their stores that reads:

> Rule 1: The customer is always right. Rule 2: If the
> customer is ever wrong, reread Rule 1.

With this in mind, off I went to our local store one evening and purchased a shrimp platter for a dinner party. Unfortunately, once opened, it was clear that something fishy was up—to be precise, the shrimp had spoiled. Thankfully, we didn't test the theory as that would have guaranteed us a bigger issue over the next 24 hours. So, the next day, I walked back into Stew Leonard's with my receipt and told the customer service worker about our disappointing dinner discovery.

"Well, do you have the platter with you?"

"Of course not! Why would I bring spoiled shrimp back into your grocery store? You would have smelled me coming!"

"Well, sir, I can't issue a refund if you don't have the product here with you."

"Well, what about your big rock out front? Does that not mean anything? I am a customer, so please refer to rule one and two!"

I was a bit surprised and, frankly, more than a bit upset. They had already contributed to a disappointing dinner party and wasted my time in having to come back to the store. I wasn't a happy customer. I continued to stand my ground. The refund was a secondary issue, really. The principle seemed worth defending. It wasn't right that they were promoting one customer experience and offering another. Eventually, they gave in to my reasoning and refunded me. But too little too late. They had caused me added distress when, in reality, I was owed an apology. Since customer experience is an area I am clearly passionate about, I went further and decided to write a letter to Stew Leonard Jr. about my disappointing interaction within one of his stores.

"Please explain why you go so far as to promote your values as if they were one of the Ten Commandments, only to ignore them completely?"

Surely, this wasn't a sign that could be misinterpreted? I ended the letter by saying that I didn't feel good as a customer. It will prohibit me from shopping there again. I received a response to my letter almost as soon as I had sent it.

Dear Mr. Boccuzzi,

We are so sorry for the experience you had relating to your shrimp. We wanted to let you know we took the following steps. Beyond the full credit on your shrimp platter, the employee that dealt with you is back in training to learn about the rock. Finally, we have enclosed a $50 gift card should you decide to give us another chance.

Thank you,

Stew Leonard Jr.

This story goes to show that good intentions are only worth the stone that they are written on. I can forgive Stew Leonard's for their mistake because they accepted responsibility and took the time to respond. Good customer service extends beyond the promise to the interpretation and delivery of that promise, which of course is part of the customer experience. The customer isn't *always* right, but they should definitely be given the benefit of the doubt when there is a strong chance that you are the ones that messed up. Don't make it difficult for customers to resolve their problems—a customer who has been wronged doesn't want to feel like they are being put on trial.

As the employer, you need to make sure you are keeping everything in balance—this is done by continually educating your employees about the morals and ethics of the company. Just like Stew Leonard Jr. did. If an employee doesn't understand or has forgotten the rules of your customer experience, then they need to be retaught—back to basics. Weekly or monthly evaluations will help eliminate employee standards slipping and prevent reputational damage that is beyond repair. The way values are interpreted may change over time, so they need to be revisited and revised as time goes on. Be mindful about how you manage this process and make sure the changes are clear and universally understood. If the customers interpret one thing and the employees another, you are on track for a major in-store bust up. To some extent, having "the customer is always right" promoted outside every one of your stores is a risky strategy. If it's not upheld consistently, then it will be seen as a gimmick and discredit the business more than it promotes it. Annual reviews won't cut it. You need to be checking in on your team every month at the very least. Rather than telling employees what your values represent, ask them to interpret those values and work from there. When their understanding matches the company's mission statement, you'll have a winning formula.

A large service provider was in the middle of building a new user interface for an insurance company. They were developing an app to help their customers calculate their renewal percentages, and part of the change was to take cost out by transitioning from a local mainframe to the cloud. This required a rebuild of the user interface (UI). Unfortunately, the UI they developed ended up being a total failure. Customers started to back out halfway through the renewal process without completing their forms. The company needed to find out why this was happening, so they employed another service provider that I was working with to help them redesign the UI. This would aid them in improving the customer experience and the completion of the insurance renewal document. This provider took a very different tactic. Rather than starting with the "cost takeout" objective mainframe to cloud, they focused first on the customer experience and UI. Using an agile approach, they created an inexpensive mock-up of how the app might work in the future. With this, they went back to a new group of panelists and asked them which interface they preferred, A or B, and why. The provider then built a full app and tied it into the cloud solution to help "optimize" cost; the conversion rate grew by 73%. So, they were able to rectify a serious issue without shelling out a fortune. A huge lesson here is that there is a major difference between "cost takeout" and "cost optimization." Whether you're using in-house resources or a third-party service provider, you need to ensure everyone is on the same page. In most cases, cost takeout will have a negative impact on experience while cost optimization will not because it always keeps experience in mind. In this case, by stopping to look at how customers were interpreting the app, they were able to develop a product that improved their customer experience and bolstered their results. The feedback from their panel survey revealed that users found some of the questions too invasive, which was causing people to bail out halfway through. At first, the insurance company's committee was hesitant to make the required changes—they didn't agree that the questions were too invasive as they were exactly the same questions that they would have asked in person. We had to remind them that an independent, remote experience wouldn't be interpreted the same as a face-to-face meeting. So, the questions needed to be adapted accordingly to be sure the customer interpreted them correctly and agreed they were valuable and relevant. Of course, many people are reluctant to give away personal information online, which feels far less secure than directly to a certified professional.

Back again to my days at Edible Arrangements. One afternoon, I overheard a customer care agent on the phone to a customer. She was apologizing a lot, so I signaled her to send the call through to me. As soon as I answered the phone, the guy blew my ear off. I could feel his hot, steaming breath puffing out through my receiver.

"I am never going to do business with you again!" he bellowed down the line.

I have learned that this is a cry for help. If they were never going to do business with you again, they probably wouldn't be on the phone with you. This was my opportunity to make amends and retain a customer.

"What is the problem you are experiencing?" I said politely. My tone of voice aimed to de-escalate the tension on his side.

He explained that he had been using the arrangements we supplied as follow-up gestures after job interviews he had been attending. Then he added that he had just lost his job on Wall Street.

I now understood why he was so angry. I'd be upset, too, if I lost a seven-figure salary.

"One of the arrangements I ordered never showed up."

As a result of his frustrations, he was acting as if the missing fruit bouquet was the reason he was unsuccessful in his job search. Of course, Wall Street doesn't trade highly paid positions for gifts—but this guy was stressed, and we had failed to deliver on our obligation. I needed to handle the situation sensitively.

He found himself with a huge financial hole to fill and was investing in our products to make the best impression he could for his potential new employers. And we dropped the ball at our end.

Recognizing that this guy was extremely on edge, I decided it was appropriate to pull out all the stops. Sure, we probably didn't wreck his employment chances, but we made a stressful experience seem that much worse.

"Well, I am a VP of this company. So why don't I give you my personal phone number? I'll be your personal concierge moving forward should you decide to give us another chance. If you need anything, you can text or call me, and I'll make sure it gets delivered."

I made the company's obligations my personal responsibility. Although this was only one customer, we had still failed him. And I wasn't going to let it happen again.

Over the next couple of days, I received a stream of messages listing what this customer wanted to send to various addresses. I then personally put every order into our system to ensure he got exactly what he ordered where he wanted it. This arrangement went very well, so well in fact, that over the next month he spent $10,000 with us. So, this was a story which began with "I am never going to do business with you again!" and ended with that very same man giving us $20,000 worth of business that year. And it was a happy ending for him, too. He eventually secured another job on Wall Street (perhaps the fruit bouquet sealed the deal).

So, I hope the message is now clear—and won't be misinterpreted. Your company's values and expectations need to align with your employee and customer expectations. Unlike all the computer programs that we use to assist us, humans will always make assumptions. So, train, check-up on, and retrain your team to ensure they remain on point and on message. Don't carve your company's values in stone if you can't guarantee they will be delivered. Make this process human-centric by asking: What is the promise? How has it been interpreted? How will this be delivered?

KEY TAKEAWAYS:

- Quick assumptions can lead to misalignment or inaccurate interpretation, as demonstrated by the story from Gallery Furniture.

- Interpretation can drift over time, so it is critical you continue to train and reinforce best practices with your team.

- Continue to monitor consumer behavior as that can shift too. You may need to make adjustments in your behavior to adapt to this.

- A misalignment in interpretation is reparable if immediately addressed, as with the Edible Arrangements story.

chapter 8

What's Next in Customer Experience?

EXPECT

As we near the end of the book, let's look to the future. Here we will consider the last "**E**" of S.E.D.U.C.E.—Expect and be ready for competitors, technology, and the market to change.

Today, and for the foreseeable future, customer experience is king. It has become the chief focus of many businesses looking to survive, develop, and grow in the modern commercial landscape. When SuperOffice asked over 1,900 business professionals their number one focus over the next five years, customer experience came out on top at 45.9% with product and pricing trailing behind. The Temkin Group found that companies that earn $1 billion annually can expect to earn, on average, an additional $700 million within three years of investing in customer experience.[29] This is because customers are taking control and demanding better experiences. The most successful online and brick-and-mortar businesses create an experience that customers want to return to again and again. When maximizing the customer experience, one of the biggest focus areas is convenience. What does delivery and pickup look like? How can customers communicate with you? What additional steps can you take to make the customer experience more seamless and frictionless? These considerations will drive better convenience and overall experience. And for many companies (including me, PwC, Temko Group, and a dozen other research and consulting firms) experience is the number one differentiator right now. In fact, according to SuperOffice, 81% of organizations already cite customer experience as a competitive differentiator.[30] This culture is a big shift from the late '90s and early 2000s, when businesses were more focused on other business levers to drive profitability.

Another reason why customer experience has become such a hot topic is because it includes environmental and social issues, which are now front and center as a priority for consumers. A term often used is environmental, social, and governance (ESG). We are now far more aware of how our shopping decisions impact the world we live in. Customers are particular about how their personal values line up with the ethics of the brands they invest in. Whether it's environmental sustainability, employment rights, or community engagement, businesses are no longer just selling products but promoting identities that define

---

29 Super Office. "32 Customer Experience Statistics You Need to Know for 2024." Accessed August 13, 2023. https://www .superoffice.com/blog/customer-experience-statistics/.

30 Super Office. "32 Customer Experience Statistics You Need to Know for 2024."

the experiences they provide. When I sat down with Lindsey Mazza, Global Retail Lead at Capgemini, a global business and technology transformation partner, she reinforced this trend and demand from customers:

> Capgemini really focuses on an "Earth to end of life" concept. It's not just the carbon footprint of the manufacturing process, it's about how the raw materials were mined, distributed, produced, transported to stores or customers, and then finally disposed of. We are very focused on the idea of being able to evaluate the full life cycle at Capgemini. From small home appliances to cosmetics, we work with clients to understand the environmental impact from Earth to end of life. It's relevant for being a purpose-driven organization, but also for profits because customers care and take notice.

The last big consumer differentiator comes in the response to the question "How does it feel to shop?" Whether it's a physical brick-and-mortar store or an online retailer—what does that shopping experience feel like to the customers? This factor, along with convenience and identity (which I already mentioned), determine whether or not a customer will make a purchase in the first place and then whether or not they will return again. Simply put, a bad shopping experience represents the likelihood of a lost opportunity. Every customer, either subconsciously or otherwise, will be asking themselves a stream of questions at each point of their customer experience. Questions like: "Did I end up getting what I needed?" "Was the experience positive?" "Was the business proactive in meeting my needs?" You get the idea. The list goes on.

Anuj Malhotra, Senior Director of Interactive at LTIMindtree explained the importance of "ecosystem thinking" that covers all affected members of the ecosystem, including consumers, partners, the enterprise, and employees at a broad level: "While transforming the digital experience of a large electronic retailer in UK, we had to think about all the channels the customer might use including responsive web, mobile and in-store sales assist app, and a customer care suite." This goes back to the concept of the "One to One Moment" we covered in chapter five. You need to be willing to meet the customer where they want to engage and then deliver a unique and personalized experience. "This personalized omni approach requires not just collaboration with your tech partners but a true design thinking approach to client challenges."

Hard to argue with Malhotra.

Customer expectations have changed rapidly over the past three years, especially in the food delivery services. Delivery times between 45 and 60 minutes used to be considered acceptable. But now, taking any more than 30 minutes will earn you a negative review. This new norm also exists outside the food delivery industry. Customers expect products to be shipped on the day they are ordered and delivered the next day, if not sooner. Technology has made us incredibly impatient. This means businesses need to ensure they have a good understanding of product demand, otherwise they risk failing their customer expectations. As a backup plan, businesses also need to understand which products can be used as a substitute or alternative offering when demand is greater than the supply of popular products. This is where artificial intelligence and machine learning can come in helpful; you can use these technologies to help anticipate demand and support customers and employees with intelligent responses to questions. This required a human with years of experience in the past. Generative AI, machine learning (ML), and large language models (LLM) will help large brands in creating an experience which is as frictionless as possible. Lindsey agreed:

> One of the most important factors that we see our retail clients focused on is fulfillment, including what delivery and pickup look like. A smoother fulfillment process creates more convenience for the consumer's lifestyle and makes it easier to use the brand. That's the number one consumer differentiator right now.

Sustainability needn't be seen as an expensive aspiration that sacrifices profit in the hope of strengthening a brand's identity. Many of the business decisions that are employed to promote sustainability can be facilitated by cost takeout measures. The key to this is increasing efficiency without sacrificing quality, speed, or customer satisfaction. Therefore, while the end goal is the shared human interest in environmentalism, the means to achieving that goal may well benefit the organization through good publicity and efficiency savings. "Affordable sustainability" has become the new mantra for customers and CEOs alike. Customers are expecting organic, healthy, and sustainable products—those that use less emissions, have a lower carbon footprint, and are made from sustainable materials such as recycled plastics, aluminum, glass, and biodegradable plastics. Generative AI and LLMs can be used here to help businesses determine the nature of customer demands, striking a balance between affordability and sustainability.

Customers are becoming increasingly aware of the impact that people are having on the planet we call home. Politics aside, the Covid-19 pandemic showed us just how much we are impacting our environment. A few months into the pandemic, photos were posted of the canals in Venice where you could actually see the floor bed with healthy green algae visible through the crystal-clear water. Smog and air pollution significantly decreased across the world. Those skeptical about the extent of human impact on the environment would now find it incredibly hard to argue that we aren't a destructive force on our planet. As a result, customers are taking far more precautions and exercising greater due diligence before spending their money. Last year, I had the chance to visit with Lindsey and others from Capgemini at one of their US innovation centers. They shared a story about a client they were working with to help them reduce the impact their small appliances (coffee makers, toaster ovens, etc.) were having on the planet. Capgemini went further than most in fighting the battle against climate change; they helped the client measure the environmental impact of mining materials, manufacturing products, consuming electricity, and disposal after use. By looking at these key areas, they were able to reduce their use of plastic and raw materials by over 30% and ultimately reduce the company's carbon footprint. Lindsey asked the questions: "How do I connect with a company's brand purpose? Does it match my personal ethos?" Then he continued with, "When my personal ethics matches the ethics of the brand that I'm working with, it drives my desire to purchase from them."

Oatly (oat milk), Allbirds (shoes), Pantys (underwear), and Tenzing (energy drink) are some of the brands leading the way in carbon footprint labeling. As the push for sustainability becomes more popular, I foresee the Federal Trade Commission creating a set of standards similar to those produced by Energy Guide to ensure that customers can source and purchase goods with a clear understanding of the environmental impact behind their choice. In Europe, there are already lots of large brands using a carbon score on their food items that outline the impact that specific item has on the environment. However, there is still lots of work yet to be done in this area. But you can count on social and environmental issues playing a huge role in customer experience in the future.

I wanted to learn more about how ESG was playing a role in employee and customer experience, so I sat down with Jason Warren, former VP Head of NetZero Transformation at Atos and current VP Head of Cross Portfolio and Analyst Relations at Atos. During our conversation, Jason shared several areas that Atos is investing in to improve the overall employee and customer experience. They were not the more traditional things you would think about when discussing customer and employee experience. For over a decade, Atos has been investing in green initiatives that not only help the environment, but their clients. Getting in early has paid off.

According to Jason:

> Atos developed a green app that helps consumers do good using gamification. Each day users are given a task to complete that is educational and helps the user do their part to make a small difference as far as being good to the environment.

> [Atos also invested in acquiring a firm, EcoAct, in 2020.] As a standalone consulting and climate advisory firm, EcoAct had a great market reputation and specifically with a strong offsetting portfolio of nature-based solutions and carbon accounting capabilities. When we acquired them, I believe we

became the first company to combine climate advisory with digital.

The transformation internally and with clients was not overnight. I had to eliminate technology acronyms and start at a place everyone could understand. I started with, this is data going on a storage device that uses power in a data center, which is this big building that has all of this technology infrastructure within it. And that's using energy, which is therefore causing emissions. From there we could start evaluating the overall emissions from digital and find ways to reduce that over time. By combining EcoAct's climate advisory expertise and best practices with our digital experience we were able to develop a new science-based commitment to clients.

A few months later, I sat down with Nourdine Bihmane, CEO of Atos. During the interview, Bihmane mentioned that the company was going through a great deal of change. But, over his 22-year career with the company, a core value has stayed with the firm. He plans to extract more of it in the future in what he called "Tech for Good." This is the same message Jason shared just a few months earlier:

We want to do right by our customers, our employees, and society, and that will be a cornerstone of the New Atos. We are the only ones in the industry committed to what we call DLA, Decarbonization Level Agreements. That means when we deliver services to a customer, we are committing from the beginning to the end of the contract to reduce our carbon footprint. If we reach our target, we are a

green supplier. If we don't reach it, I am committing
the company to compensate the customer with carbon credit offsets to make sure at the end of the day
Atos in your supply chain is a green supplier.[31]

Over the next few years, other service providers and technology firms will either acquire climate advisory firms or create their
own to support customer demands to be kinder to the environment as they make large digital enhancements. Climate impact
will absolutely be part of the conversation going forward when
thinking about customer experience. Customers and employees
want to do business with companies that have an eye on their
carbon footprint and the environment. Will DLAs become the
norm in a few years? My money is on "YES." Atos is showing the
industry the art of the possible when it comes to committing to
decarbonization. In my opinion, it's even leading the way. I can't
wait to see what's next.

AI and ML will allow companies to learn more about their
customer, how they buy, why they buy, what they want, and
what they dislike or no longer desire. For many, the thought
of companies knowing even more about you as a person is
scary. Companies such as Facebook and TikTok have already
stoked a lot of controversy by harvesting and selling our data
and by analyzing our every move online, which feels invasive to
say the least. However, I don't believe there's any reason to lose
any sleep yet. The bottom line is that in order to connect more
personally with a customer, a business needs to know your likes
and dislikes. This doesn't necessarily mean that they need your
search history or will want to read your personal messages. If the

---

31 YouTube. "ISG Interview with Nourdine Bihmane." Accessed
August 1, 2023. https://www.youtube.com/watch?v=OY0pi1K-c6Y.

goal is to create a more personalized experience, then have at it. Take Oreo, for example. They have created a website that allows customers to personalize their packaging and the cookie itself. You can now have a loved one's face etched into your cookie— something you didn't realize you needed, but plenty seem happy to spend their money on them. Without a good understanding of each customer, the experience is limited to off-the-shelf products and procedures. The market has moved on rapidly from that level of engagement. In the uber-competitive world of commerce, companies are now using technology to facilitate cost optimization and sustainability, better understand revenue growth streams, and recommend new products to meet new needs.

Personally, I love the thought of hyperpersonalization. I met with Harish Pai, CTO of Infinite, a large technology firm that focuses on providing solutions to the healthcare sector. Pai shared some of the challenges insurance companies (payers) and hospitals, clinics, and doctors (providers) are struggling with today including personalization and the "one to one moment." He said:

> The ability to deliver hyperpersonalized experiences
> to patients by better using data and technology
> including generative AI is going to change the way
> care is provided to patients.

Today, payers pay providers by incident. You go to the hospital for a condition, and the provider pays a portion of that visit to the provider. Payers want to move to a "value-based care" model where the payer now pays a fee by condition not by visit. This can be a risk for providers, but it can also be an opportunity to deliver a better long-term patient experience that is more profitable.

This may sound like the payers are trying to hand off responsibility to providers. Maybe they are, but there is an opportunity for providers to deliver a hyperpersonalized and seamless omni-channel experience to patients to help them stay healthy, which overall reduces costly visits. The other major outcome is a better patient experience.

According to Harish:

> Who wants to spend time going in and out of health-care facilities? We are creating the tools for payers that they can offer to provider groups, saying, "Sign up with us and we will provide you a set of tools you can use to more effectively manage your patients and create better patient experiences and outcomes."

I asked Harish if the value-based model would create a better patient experience. The answer was "yes."

> As a patient, I am now starting to lead a much bet-ter lifestyle because somebody is coaching me on a constant basis and sending me relevant articles for my condition. It's a great example of proactive and predictive customer experience if done right.

What about designing your own custom pair of Nike sneakers now that your health provider has shared that you need to exercise more? Yep, Nike launched "Nike by you" to do just that. You can choose key features including the color of each part of the sneaker and even add an embroidered message. However, personalization doesn't always mean manufacturing something. Think about Spotify or Netflix. Both provide personalized playlists or suggested watching as the system gets to know your tastes better. In 2021, McKinsey & Company asked consumers which areas of person-alization mattered to them most. The top three were: make it easy for me to navigate in store or online; give me relevant product and service recommendations; tailor the messaging to my needs.

To put the significance of personalized customer experience for your business in numbers:

- McKinsey & Company: "Companies that excel at personalization generate 40% more revenue from those activities than average players."

- HubSpot: "Personalized call-to-actions convert 202% better than default versions."

- 123 Form Builder: "90% of customers are willing to spend more when companies provide personalized customer services."

- Accenture Research: "91% of consumers are more likely to shop with brands that recognize, remember, and provide them with relevant offers and recommendations."

- In 2022, "61% of customers would leave for a competitor after just one negative experience" up from "48% of all consumers" in 2018 (123 Form Builder & Accenture Research).[32]

Since 2020, the consumer market has evolved rapidly. Millennials and GenZers are no longer children but adults with disposable incomes. Businesses who have maintained the same practices for the last century need to rapidly reevaluate their offering to ensure they are keeping up with the market they serve. For the first time in consumer history, young adults are spending more than saving. Ignoring this change will be deadly

---

32 Calvelo, Manuel. "Examples of Customer Experience Personalization." Simplea. Accessed August 11, 2023. https:// simplea.com/Articles/examples-personalization.

for businesses. These generations have transformed the way that they shop and have reassessed their priorities while navigating the shopping experience. For example, they put a great deal of research into the foods they feed their families, the products they put on their bodies, the items they bring into their homes, and even the emissions that were spent in manufacturing those items. Businesses need to recognize, understand, and respond to the new ethics of shopping culture to ensure they are not alienating a group of customers with huge spending power. The saying goes that "the customer is always right"—and this must not be forgotten; businesses need to walk in the shoes of the people they serve. With the products and services markets more competitive than ever, it is no longer good enough to take the attitude that "you'll take the products that we sell, and that's that." In this respect, personalization is just as much about recognizing the needs of a generation (or two) as much as it is about catering to the needs of individuals.

In the ever-evolving landscape of customer experience, a prominent trend that will shape the coming years is the transition toward proactive and predictive strategies. Traditional customer service models have typically been reactive, where companies wait for customers to initiate contact with their concerns or requests. However, with the rapid advancements in technology and the increasing availability of data analytics, businesses now have the power to anticipate customer needs and address them proactively. The concept of a proactive customer experience involves identifying potential issues or opportunities and acting before customers even realize they require assistance. With this insight, businesses can proactively implement targeted retention campaigns or deliver personalized offers, effectively mitigating the risk of customer attrition. An example of proactive customer experience is the utilization of notifications and alerts. By analyzing customer data, companies can preemptively identify potential issues or disruptions in the customer journey, enabling them to promptly notify customers about relevant information. For example, an airline might notify passengers about flight delays or gate changes through mobile apps or text messages to prevent frustration at the airport gate. This not only empowers customers to adjust their plans accordingly but showcases the company's commitment to delivering a seamless experience, even if they do have to wait slightly longer before jetting off on holiday.

Proactive customer experience extends beyond issue resolution. It anticipates issues before they have happened and meets them with recommendations and suggestions. While good issue resolution may prevent a customer from taking their business elsewhere, preventing the issue from happening in the first place will offer a greater chance of customer retention. When issues are predictable, they are preventable, and preventable issues are those which irk customers the most.

By thoroughly analyzing customer data and gaining insights into their preferences, companies can offer highlypersonalized recommendations and suggestions for products or services that customers may find valuable. Therefore, as well as enhancing the shopping experience, personalization also helps boost sales revenue. It is all very good and well to offer excellent customer service, but that's of no use to a customer if they are unaware that you sell the goods they desire. Don't allow the customer the opportunity to overlook your offering. Capture their attention before they take their money elsewhere.

This proactive approach not only resolves concerns swiftly, but it fosters a sense of trust and loyalty among customers who feel like the business is invested in getting to know them and their individual needs. Looking ahead, the trajectory of proactive and predictive customer experience appears promising. Companies will continue to invest in technology, including generative AI, aiming to refine their ability to anticipate customer needs, provide personalized recommendations, and take proactive actions. By embracing this progressive mindset, businesses can forge ahead in the competitive marketplace, delivering exceptional experiences that surpass customer expectations and drive sustainable growth. It's a win-win, folks.

There are many parts of the customer experience that can be improved by using AI to enhance the way businesses can interact with their customers. As of May 2023, the most popular are OpenAI's GPT-4, Google's PaLM2, Microsoft CoPilot, and Meta's LLaMA. Where previously, customers would have spent hours on the phone listening to terrible hold music, generative AI can now step in and put everyone to the front of the queue. By allowing generative AI to support human work forces, businesses have increased capacity to provide a quick turnaround on troubleshooting and problem resolution. This is facilitated by "conversational AI" that is able to ask customers pertinent questions and, in many instances, diagnose and resolve issues without the need for human intervention. In some ways, the AI is more effective than real-life customer service, as they ask multiple questions at once and retain that information so customers no longer have to suffer human error and repeat themselves.

Part of the challenge with AI is it is only as strong as the data used to educate the AI system. That could mean disparate data sets that are over 40 years old sitting on mainframes or in data centers. Although AWS, Google, and Microsoft may disagree, not everything needs to be in the cloud. In most cases, leveraging data on mainframes and data centers is not only cost-effective but far more efficient, secure, and reliable than if it was moved to the cloud. I learned a lot about how to get the most from your legacy and current data from Bryan Doerr at Ensono.

According to Bryan Doerr:

> Clients are asking us to not only support them with new software and new application delivery models that include the hyperscalers, but to make sure that they have the right interfaces, the right data availability, the right data positioning and grooming so they can leverage that data. These disparate data sets might exist in dozens of locations including data centers and mainframes. To create the most personalized experience for customers, you need all the data regardless of location. Not everything needs or should be moved to the cloud. Helping to modernize foundational systems and data is what Ensono hangs its hat on.

I encourage you to not make quick decisions when it comes to modernizing your systems to save money or leverage AI. Ask questions, get second and third opinions, include a third-party advisor, and read the latest research on the topic. Over the last few years, I have seen far too many large businesses rush to move everything to the cloud only to fail.

In early 2023, I had the opportunity to meet with Madhava Reddy, founder and CEO of HTC Global Services, along with some of his executive team, in their headquarters in Detroit. They provide business services, including digital engineering and design. Founded in 1990, they have been creating unique solutions for large enterprise clients ever since. One such solution was for a large auto insurance company. They devised a system where if a policy holder was in an accident, they could quickly call for assistance, including a tow truck and transportation away from the accident site. By taking a few photos of the car using their app, the insurance company can quickly estimate the repairs, find and connect the tow truck with the closest repair shop, facilitate the payment, and ensure the car can be fixed without unnecessary delay. HTC also worked with a large entertainment park in Orlando to design a new training module for a large ride that required staff to know facts about dozens of animals that were part of the ride. Traditionally, this was done by having the employees travel on the ride several times to learn about the animals and the overall experience. The challenge was there were thousands of employees, so this was not only time consuming but took up space on the ride that was meant for paying guests. HTC Global Services spent time with the client in their innovation center and on the ride and proposed a virtual reality solution that allowed employees to experience the ride without having to actually be on the ride. It was very immersive and provided the ability for employees to drill down on specific animals during the ride to learn more details. The result was a far more efficient and cost-effective approach to training that also opened up thousands of seats on the ride for paying guests, reducing wait times. A win all the way around.

Digital twin is another technology that will assist with customer experience soon. This technology allows businesses to create digital replicas of anything from a shopper to a coffee maker. They can then run a simulation and test different scenarios with the replica designed to mimic the behaviors of qualities of the real thing as closely as possible. It all sounds very sci-fi, but watch this space and start reading more about the topic—being one of the first adopters of this technology may be a game-changing move for your business and allow you to deliver a near-to-immaculate customer experience. By way of example, you may be a car manufacturer. By creating a digital replica of the car's components, you can test the wear and tear of essential parts under different scenarios. This would allow you to determine areas for product development and manage the supply of replacement parts. Or, if you work in retail, you might run scenarios on how a shopper may navigate their way around your store. This will give insight on optimal layout, display design, and aisle flow. And of course, all of this enhances the customer experience.

As we enter the post pandemic era where more and more of our services are facilitated by front-end technology solutions, such as mobile and website applications, the need to join this up with back-end data is becoming greater. What does this mean? Well, enterprises have spent a great deal of time on enhancing mobile apps and websites, and the user experience continues to get easier. The next big jump is to connect this front-end experience with mid- and back-office data, including inventory and location data. This will allow businesses to better connect the online and in-store experiences, including curbside pickup or even supply chain controls. The pandemic taught us a lot about the importance of supply chains. For example, we learned that if a car manufacturer is missing just one chip, they can't manufacture their car.[33] If you are not including your CIO, CDO, CMO, CHRO, CFO, and heads of supply chain, procurement and customer care in executive level conversations, you are setting yourself up to have gaps in the experience.

---

33 Adams, Keith. "Global Chip Shortage: Mercedes CEO on 'COVID Whiplash.'" Car Magazine. Accessed August 14, 2023. https://www.carmagazine.co.uk/car-news/industry-news/global-chip-shortage/.

As discussed earlier, the late '90s and early 2000s were focused on cost take-out to boost profits. This could include manufacturing overseas, moving call centers to less expensive locations around the world, and building dependencies with fewer suppliers to gain volume discounts. This worked until the world shut down (literally). All of a sudden, we needed our supply chains and call centers to be closer and more diverse. On March 10, 2020, I was presenting in NYC at ISG's Future of Work Summit. I was discussing trends that we could expect to see over the next three to five years. Little did I know, a few days later, New York City and then most of the US and world would shut down completely. What we thought would happen over the next three to five years happened over the next three to five days!

With so much uncertainty in the world, it is crucial to involve a larger leadership team when making decisions that may impact the employee or customer experience. CFOs need to be available to offer a view on cost savings, while CDOs and CIOs can share ideas on how technology can improve the experience. The head of procurement and CIO should be finding ways to reduce risk that could negatively impact your experience. Simply put, decisions need to be more inclusive moving forward. The aftermath of the Covid-19 outbreak made this very apparent.

The future of customer experience will be grounded in data. The quicker you embrace this, the more future-proof your business will be. As a friction hunter, you need to integrate and develop all your departments into your data system. This transition will not be easy on employees or customers, so it is crucial to have a clear roadmap and design a strong organizational change management process to make it as seamless as possible for all those concerned.

History suggests that the "customer experience" started at least as early as 2000 BC in a small city called Pompeii. There was no technology and, in most cases, a sole proprietor and purely local customers. Today, the customer experience is dominated by technological developments, as the local patrons have been replaced by a global customer base. Many family-owned businesses, which have grown over generations and pride themselves on the maintenance of traditional practices, may be reluctant to embrace the digital era. However, while you can maintain goods and values that are born out of tradition, the experience must now be facilitated by data-driven computer technologies behind the scenes if you want to compete at the highest level.

Of course, I had to ask ChatGPT what it thought about the future of delivering the best possible customer experience. This is what it said:

For companies to achieve a successful omnichannel experience for their consumers, they will need to follow this list:

1. **Channel Integration:** Businesses must create a unified customer experience across all their channels. This means ensuring consistent branding, messaging, and user interfaces across different touchpoints such as apps, websites, and brick-and-mortar stores. Companies should invest in robust CRM systems and APIs to facilitate real-time data sharing and synchronization between various systems.

2. **Data-Driven Insights:** Companies could leverage customer data from different channels to gain actionable insights. Businesses can better understand customer needs and tailor their offerings by analyzing data, such as customer behavior, preferences, and

purchase history. Data analytics and AI-powered tools
will play a more prominent role in extracting valuable
insights from large volumes of customer data. Don't
be a late adopter.

3. **Personalization at Scale:** Personalization will
   continue to be a key focus area in the omnichannel
   landscape. Companies can use AI and ML algorithms
   to create highly personalized experiences for
   individual customers. This includes personalized
   recommendations, targeted marketing campaigns,
   and customized interactions based on customer
   preferences and previous interactions.

4. **Mobile Optimization:** With the growing popularity
   of mobile devices, businesses need to prioritize mobile
   optimization to provide a seamless experience for
   customers on smartphones and tablets. Mobile apps
   should be designed to offer intuitive navigation,
   fast loading times, and personalized content. Also,
   technologies like location-based services enable
   companies to deliver location-specific offers and
   recommendations to mobile users.

5. **Enhanced Customer Support:** As part of the
   omnichannel experience, companies should invest in
   comprehensive customer support solutions. This can
   include chatbots and virtual assistants for self-service,
   live chat for real-time assistance, and integration of
   support channels for a consistent experience. The goal
   is to provide customers with multiple avenues to seek
   help and resolve issues promptly.

While speaking with the Global Lead of Retail at Capgemini, Lindsey Mazza, she had similar feedback regarding the importance and move to true omnichannel experiences:

> In the past we talked about omnichannel, but really it was location data. With better tools to collect and analyze location data including generative AI, it's less about knowing information from different locations and more about connecting the dots for customers based on that data and where they are at the moment (in store, online, or in the metaverse). For example, "I saw that you bought this online last week, and this is the belt that goes with it." Or "this is the accompanying hair product that goes with a shampoo you bought online if you're inside a mass merchant," for instance. This is knowing the customer at a personal level, and knowing where they might purchase next. That's the difference between making it multichannel and making it truly omnichannel.

Hard to argue, right?

So where does this all leave us and what have we learned?

KEY TAKEAWAYS:

- Customer experience is a priority in the minds of businesses and will be for at least the next five years. If you are looking for ways to invest in your business to drive differentiation, revenue, and profits, then invest in enhancing the customer experience.

- Generative AI and LLM is not a fad and will quickly and forever change the way we create employee and customer delight. Find small projects where you and your team can quickly build success and then expand this to other areas of the business.

- To create the best customer and employee experience and avoid risk, you will need to be more inclusive. Technology is no longer just for the CIO. Technology now impacts so many areas you need to ensure all stakeholders are involved and onboard. Convenient and friction free experiences, identity including ESG and overall feeling of a consumer when integrating with your company or brand, will be areas of focus when integrating new technology and data to improve customer experience.

Conclusion

We can thank our antecedents for a lot of the customer experience techniques we employ today, whether that be the painted food vessels which preceded modern-day branding and package design, the vision of Neiman Marcus in the early 1900s that centered their whole business model around the customer experience, or the insights of Lou Carborne who was the first to formalize the concept of "customer experience" in 1994. Despite this wealth of guidance before us, many businesses still choose to ignore the lessons of history and continue to put profit first. Ironically, by doing this, they are almost ensuring that their business will go down in history as just another warning against neglecting the customer experience.

As well as developing many of the practices we use today, history also reminds us of what *not* to do when offering a customer experience. Sears, Kodak, JC Penney, and Blockbuster Video are all examples of where ignoring the customer experience led to the downfall of once great businesses. What have we learned?

1. **Sears**—Be on the lookout for competitors that are offering a solution with less friction. Don't sacrifice

quality including customer service for short-term gains. Your customer will notice this and quickly desert you when an alternative is presented. In this case, Amazon.

2. **Kodak**—Don't deny your customer the best product/service available. Sitting on good ideas is never clever. Eventually, someone will beat you to it and customer loyalty only goes so far when a rival has something better to offer.

3. **JC Penney**—Don't change your business structure overnight. Even the most loyal customer is going to jump ship if you take away the concept they have invested in. Change is best when implemented incrementally and through a process that engages your customer base and is in line with expectations of the market.

4. **Blockbuster Video**—It doesn't matter how much of the market you dominate, there is never room for complacency as markets are rapidly changing in the digital era. Embrace any new technology that enhances customer convenience, or you'll find yourself pushed out by ambitious new companies.

Whether ancient or modern, history offers us huge insights into the best way to manage customer experiences. While you should avoid the mistakes listed above, there are plenty of examples of businesses that have built their success on the back of providing an excellent customer experience. In this book, I have provided you with examples from single-shop retailers to world-leading megabrands. It really doesn't matter how big or small your business is, you cannot afford to neglect your customers. In the twenty-first century, the customer is truly king, as they have been empowered by more choice than ever before. Even the best products will sit on shelves collecting dust if the customer they target isn't invested in the whole experience.

Take my friend Ruth, for example. You'll remember that she owns a single store in New York called 10/10 Optics. Thankfully, I stumbled across her when in need of some new frames, and because of her attention to detail and focus on the customer experience, I have never looked back. Ruth is successful despite being dwarfed by massive chains selling frames at a lower cost, including Warby Parker. Her success lies in the fact that she doesn't just sell eyeglasses, she sells memories too. And don't forget Arnob's 17-year-old daughter's comment. "It needs to be memorable." There's also Jack Mitchell, who is now my go-to for suits and menswear. The brands he carries may cost a bit more than the market average, and yet I (and plenty of others) keep going back. This goes to show you that having the cheapest product or brand isn't going to guarantee you success. Customers are willing to pay a little extra for the right experience. There is an exception—the promise of no-frills but unbeatable prices, which the likes of Walmart have mastered. But this only works because their customer base have bought into the concept before they have entered the store. So, when designing and implementing the customer experience in your business, first put yourself in the shoes of your customer. What do they expect and where will they be open to trade-offs? If you're a luxury brand, learn from the luxury brands you yourself admire. As a consumer, if your unique selling point is unbeatable value, consider the experiences offered by the big players in this market.

It is one thing to learn from the best, but it is another to then implement these successful practices into our own business. You cannot expect to offer the best customer experience unless you employ an amazing team to support you. The focus on customer experience needs to be placed at every level of your organization from the top executives down to the factory floor or shop counter. If any layer of your business is not engaged in providing the best customer experience, the end result will fall short of what is expected. Remember Ron Johnson, the Apple executive who took over the wheel at JC Penney and made a tough situation far worse? This happened because he completely overlooked his customers when he devised his plan for redevelopment. On the flip side, if you have an executive team that has incorporated customer-focus into their core values, this cannot be delivered if those lower down the ladder aren't themselves invested in the mission. This was illustrated by my disappointing shopping experience at Stew Leonard's supermarket and their big old rock (which could have been misleading) that claimed "the customer is always right." The store associate in this story wasn't interpreting the core values properly, and the company was left with egg on their face. However, sometimes the employees cannot be to blame; if you don't empower your customer-facing staff to facilitate excellent experiences, then the words in your mission statement may as well be written in invisible ink. It wasn't good enough that I had to write to the owner before I was compensated for my spoiled shrimp platter. Too little too late. (To be fair, Stew Jr. did recover by writing a very personal note and ensuring me the employee was back in training to learn about the rock and what it meant.) Instead, follow the example of the New York New York Hotel in Las Vegas. After my tiresome day in airport queues and cramped plane seats, the receptionist who greeted me was able to act with generosity and kindness in offering me a free upgrade to a bigger room. She didn't need to do this; they were not at fault for my grumpiness. But this kindness was possible because she didn't need to seek permission from her higher-ups before granting such a gesture. Overall, this was a great investment on their part. They filled an otherwise empty room and earned themselves a shout-out in my book and a lifelong patron of their hotel.

You get the point. Employees matter. The customer experience depends on them. Of course, your super "Team of Ruths" cannot be plucked out of thin air, which is why the hiring process is discussed in this book. Simply put, the hiring process should reflect everything and everyone in your company (if you feel you've read that before, you're right; it was in chapter three). JetBlue was the poster boy for great recruitment with their initiative to hire first responders as flight attendants. Moving on from *who* you hire, you must also think about *how* you hire. Google offered a great example with their "humanized" interview process that focuses on the character and values of their future employees. By choosing their successful candidates from those whose nature matches their company values, the core ethics of the company can trickle down to the customer experience.

The final takeaway on recruitment is to expand at a modest pace. A decent recruitment program won't handle the pressure of a mass influx of new hires. Sure, profits may go up if you expand your workforce at record rates, but the quality of your output is likely to go down. The bottom line is an inferior customer experience.

Another way to implement best practices is by investing in your target market *before* they are customers. Investing in the experience of *potential customers* is the easiest way of converting them from window shoppers to happy spenders. Whether you are pitching to an investment bank or selling pastries on Main Street, the pre-customer experience is essential for building your numbers. Your pre-sale experience should communicate to potential customers, "we are invested in your needs." This message can be facilitated by personalized marketing that delivers one-to-one advertising campaigns to individuals. The logic is simple. Demonstrate that respect to your target market, and they'll feel more impelled to invest in you. This is of course made easier by generative AI and data.

When developing your customer experience, you need to think about not only what you can give but also what you can take away. This is where you need to assume the role of a friction hunter. If you have a decent product or service, chances are you'll have competitors on your toes, hoping to snatch up some of your market share. This is why you cannot afford to be complacent, even when you are at the top. You don't want to end up like Blockbuster who scoffed at the idea of DVDs by post, only to be overtaken by Netflix who have built their success on providing ever-better convenience to their customers. Whether it be Disney's FastPass or Starbucks's remote ordering application, improving the ease and convenience of your customer's experience is a winning formula.

Technology has provided many of the answers needed to facilitate frictionless experiences. And it will play a big part in the future of customer experience, as I summarized in the previous chapter. As this is likely to be fresh in your memory, I won't repeat myself too much here, but I do want to stress that the sooner you embrace generative AI and incorporate it into your business the better. I also suggest you invest in outside resources that are focused on this area to assist you. We can't be experts in everything and must know when to leverage outside experts to assist. Start small, get some quick wins, and then expand. Technology exists that allows you to respond effectively to customers without so much as picking up a phone or tapping a keyboard. The customer experience isn't compromised but rather improved as conversational AI allows for infinite and immediate response times, regardless of the people-power available to you. This isn't a replacement for face-to-face communication, which of course adds a warmer touch. It is a supplement that increases your chances of meeting satisfied customers rather than those at the end of their tether.

So where does this leave us? Well, in order to win customers over and keep them coming back, you must first S.E.D.U.C.E. them!

- **Step** up and pay attention.

- **Employ** and empower the best teams with experience in mind.

- **Design** experience not just for retention but also acquisition.

- **Uncover** friction and resolve.

- **Connect** the dots between intention and expectation.

- **Expect** competitors, technology, and the market to change and be ready for it.

As this book reaches its conclusion, I am going to transport you back to where we began our journey—Italy. I can't think of a better place to leave you, with the sun beating down, smells of fresh Mediterranean cooking filling the air, and classical beauty decorating the streets and buildings around us. You may remember that my family enjoyed a vacation in Italy that included a visit to Pompeii a few years ago. The experience was so memorable in such a wonderful way that I feel it's worth sharing with you again.

We had spent the day touring the sites of Pompeii, taking in the magnificent scenery and enriching ourselves in ancient history. Talk of all the street food vendors turned our attention to dinner. My sister Marie had done a Google search prior to leaving the US and booked the experience. A very different experience than 2,000 years ago in Pompeii. As we drove up the Amalfi Coast to Sorrento, we stopped at a small lemon farm owned by an elderly Italian woman who spoke very little English. Thankfully, her son was on hand to translate. He explained that he had developed the family business to offer a "farm to table" experience. Prior to enjoying an amazing meal, the son took us for a tour of the farm. After the tour, we went back to the farmhouse and were seated for dinner. It is important to remember that an excellent experience doesn't always have to come with bells and whistles. The food we were served was simple, but beautifully so. We had crushed tomatoes and fresh lemon juice from the farm poured over calamari—everything came from their land or the nearby sea, through their hands and onto our plate. Homegrown and homemade, with local produce that probably made up much of the diet of the residents of ancient Pompeii 2,000 years ago. So, in this case, the simplicity made for an exceptional experience. All of our five senses were entertained that evening, from the texture of the freshly grown vegetables and the taste of the organic lemons to the smells and sounds of the nature around us and the view of the ocean ahead. It was truly magical, not in a Disney way, but a memorable experience all the same.

From the first examples of customer experience practiced by early civilizations to the present-day world of artificial intelligence, the art of creating an experience has come a long way. But, at the heart of the matter, nothing has changed. Customer experiences are designed and facilitated to give businesses a competitive edge in their market. Whether you were an ancient Italian selling snail soup out of terracotta pots or you're a global tech brand redefining consumerism in the 21st century by selling more than a product or service—by selling an experience—you become a trader in positive memories. Then, you are likely to be rewarded with customer loyalty and market-share security within your industry. Was the investment to S.E.D.U.C.E. our customers worth it? The only way to truly find out for yourself is to start the process and see what happens! I assure you, you will be happy you did.

Acknowledgments

Amazing how selecting a pair of frames in a small optic store in NYC would lead to a friendship, TEDx talk at Bryant University, and now a book.

First and foremost, I want to thank my wife, Cynthia. Meeting you in June of 1995 was the catalyst for what I can only describe as an incredible life with many more fun chapters to write together. Without even trying, you continually motivate me to be the best version of myself. I love you more than yesterday but less than tomorrow.

To my two amazing children, Sabrina and John III. Thanks to you two, I am a dad and a very lucky one at that. Your smiles, laughs, motivation, and joy for life put a smile on my face each day. Sabrina, thank you for offering to be my editor. Your feedback and suggestions were invaluable, and I could not have done it without you. To my mom and dad, who taught me what amazing experiences in life look like, including our trips to Disney. Financially, we may not have been a wealthy family, but thanks to you two and my amazing sister Marie, our lives were, and continue to be, rich!

Special thanks to my incredible team that helped me get this book from an idea to print. Holly Hudson, thanks for listening to all my stories and helping me put those thoughts into words. Rachel Valliere, your cover and book design transformed my words into art. It's a reminder that a great story is even better with great design. Thank you, Katya Fishman, for being my expert on everything publishing. You gave me dozens of things to think about, and it truly enhanced the entire experience and end product.

To all the executives that gave me their time over the last nine months to discuss customer and employee experience and why each is so important to build and grow thriving teams, loyal customers, and profitable businesses. Special thanks to Scott Taylor, who gave me the kick in the pants I needed to get my book started. Once I was off the starting line, there was no stopping me. Thank you, Chris Ragot. I feel so fortunate that we met in 1999 on a random business flight home from Tennessee. Your friendship, advice, and mentoring have been invaluable over the years. My life is richer because of you. You helped me understand what great leadership looks like and reinforced the importance of customer and employee experience when building a business. Special thanks to Janet Ursone, my first boss after college. Your patience and mentoring helped set the foundation for my leadership style, and for that I am truly grateful.

Finally, to Ruth Domber-Rozenberg, the owner of 10/10 Optics, who changed the way I looked at myself and the world. You helped me focus on what really matters in business, customer experience. You seduced me as a customer over 25 years ago, and I have never looked back.

About the Author

John Boccuzzi Jr. has been making a positive impact in business across sales, marketing, and customer experience leadership roles for over twenty-five years. His TEDx talk "I was Seduced by Exceptional Customer Service" was ranked the most popular video to learn customer experience lessons from by Omoto in 2018, and one of the best customer service training videos online by HubSpot in 2021.

Early in his career, John became fascinated by how impactful exceptional customer experience can be on a business. From his early days at small local businesses to larger enterprises like Edible Arrangements, where he supported over 1,200 franchised locations and millions of customers in North America, John has always put customer and employee experience first.

John has worked on delivering exceptional customer experiences with some of the largest manufacturers, retailers, software providers, and agencies in the world including Amazon, Ahold, Atos, Genpact, LTIMindtree, Heineken, IBM, Bacardi, Procter & Gamble, GSK and Pfizer, Google, Shutterfly, Café Press, Fandango, T-Mobile, David's Bridal, Destination Maternity,

The Children's Place, General Mills, Colgate, Heinz, GE, Nestle Purina, and Verizon.

He is currently a partner and sits on the executive board as the president of ISG Research, one of the largest research and advisory firms globally, cohost of the *John & Ola* podcast, and cofounder of BD Provisions, a specialty bulk food and coffee roasting house that is now being franchised across the United States.

John gives keynotes and facilitates workshops about how to deliver exceptional customer experience around the globe.

When John is not roasting coffee at BD Provisions, hosting a podcast, or giving a keynote on customer experience, he enjoys spending time with his two amazing children and his incredible wife, Cynthia.

Bonus Content

Want another story of exceptional customer experience with tips that apply to any industry?

Scan the QR code below to get a free download of
6 Lessons in Customer Experience from a Cheesemonger

"John captured the entire audience, personally relating to the different individuals during our annual owner's meeting and transformed their perspective on investments in customer experience and the anticipated ROI."
—Simone Vingerhoets-Ziesmann,
Executive Vice President, Ligne Roset Americas

Book John for your next big meeting, conference, customer event, podcast, or sales kickoff

John Boccuzzi Jr. is asked to speak in front of audiences of five to 5,000 on topics related to customer and employee experience and how each can have a significant impact on a business's revenue and bottom line.

John is also available as an emcee for special events recognizing customers, clients, and/or employees.

He has hosted over 100 podcasts covering technology, customer experience, and how businesses can differentiate themselves.

GET IN TOUCH

john@boccuzzillc.com
https://www.linkedin.com/in/johnboccuzzi/

Book an appointment:

https://boccuzzillc.com/book-an-appointment

"John delivered an exceptional presentation. Our owners were engaged the entire time and walked away with a new enlightenment on customer experience. The information was so valuable in reminding all of us how we make our guest feel is so crucial to our success."
—Evonne Vardy, Cofounder, Clean Eatz